SINGER®
Sewing Custom Curtains, Shades, *and* Top Treatments

Quarto is the authority on a wide range of topics.

Quarto educates, entertains and enriches the lives of our readers—enthusiasts and lovers of hands-on living.

www.QuartoKnows.com

© 2016 Quarto Publishing Group USA Inc.
Illustrations © 2016 Susan Woodcock

First published in the United States of America in 2016
by Creative Publishing international, an imprint of Quarto Publishing Group USA Inc.
400 First Avenue North
Suite 400
Minneapolis, MN 55401
1-800-328-3895
QuartoKnows.com
Visit our blogs at QuartoKnows.com

10 9 8 7 6 5 4 3 2 1

ISBN: 978-1-58923-931-9

Digital edition published in 2016
eISBN: 978-1-63159-155-6

Library of Congress Cataloging-in-Publication Data available

Cover Image: Susan Woodcock
Design and Page Layout: Laura Shaw Design, Inc.
Photography: Susan Woodcock
Illustration: Susan Woodcock

Printed in China

SINGER®
SEWING CUSTOM
Curtains, Shades, and Top Treatments

A Complete Step-by-Step Guide to Making and Installing Window Décor

SUSAN WOODCOCK

Creative Publishing international

Contents

Introduction

Interior decoration is an important part of every home. Soft furnishings like curtains, bedding, and upholstery can create beautiful rooms filled with pattern, color, and texture. But there is also a practical side. Fabric furnishings can improve your quality of living, making your home inviting, safe, and comfortable.

Creating your own window coverings can be very rewarding. You will feel accomplished and proud of your skills, and save money. That is not to say that making your own window treatments is cheap. The fabric, supplies, and hard-ware that you will need to complete your project can be a big investment. But if you are willing to devote the time and effort to planning and making them properly, your window treatments will last for many, many years. Money well spent!

This book is designed to give you added confidence as you learn basic to advanced skills. With each new project you will gain experience and soon you will be able to tackle any type of window treatment.

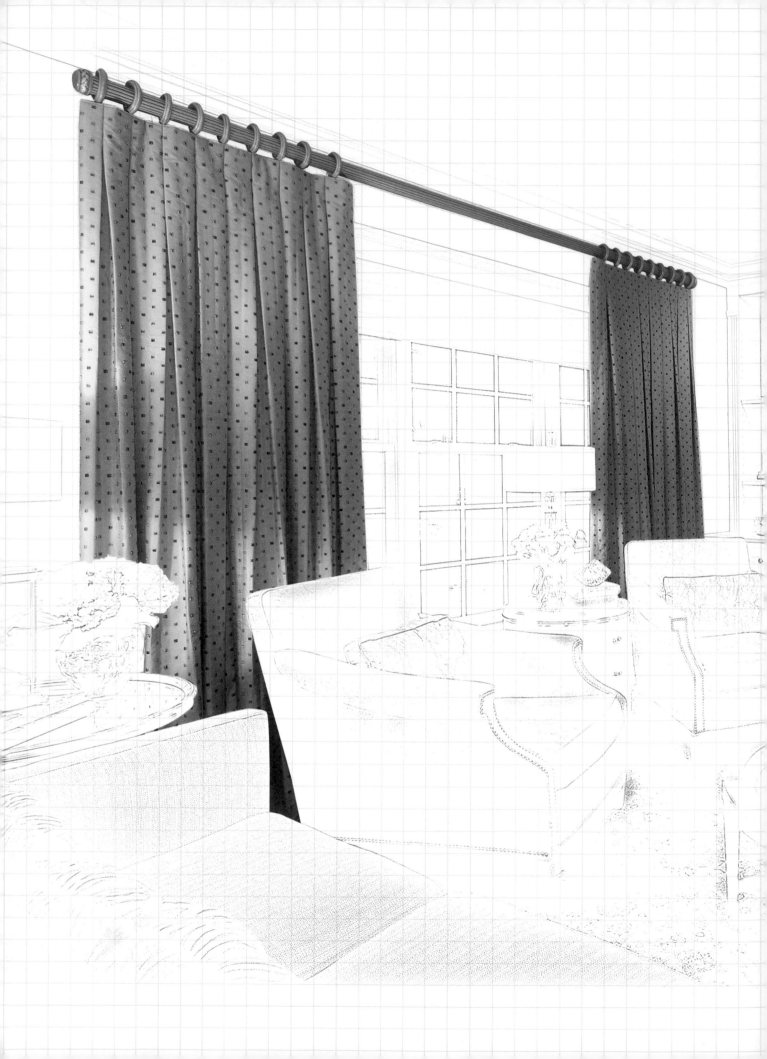

PLANNING YOUR PROJECT

Designing and selecting window treatments is a big job, and there are many decisions to make along the way. This book will guide you through the process from measuring to finishing touches. Begin by looking for inspiration in books, magazines, and websites and researching the tools, materials, and supplies needed to complete the project, and then follow along with the how-to instructions to create custom designs for your windows.

Identifying Styles

There are two categories of window treatments: *hard* (shutters, horizontal and vertical blinds) and *soft* (draperies, curtains, valances). Soft window treatments are composed of four basic styles: flat, gathered, pleated, and swagged. Elements of each are combined to create a wide variety of unique designs.

Flat styles of window treatments include Roman shades and cornice boards where the fabric is hanging or stretched flat. Grommet and tab-top curtains are made without any pleats and are flat panels of fabric before being put on the rod.

Gathered styles have fullness; extra fabric is figured into the width, and is then shirred onto a rod with a pocket sewn into the top or gathered up with sew-on tapes.

This Roman shade is an example of a flat style.

This gathered curtain is made with a rod pocket. Extra fabric above the rod creates a pretty ruffle at the top.

On pleated styles, extra fabric is divided into uniform sections. The pleated sections can be on the front or reverse side of the window treatment. Pleats can be flat and plain like a box pleat, or formed into decorative soft shapes, as in goblet, French, or butterfly pleat styles.

To create swag styles, the fabric is draped so that it falls on the bias, or diagonal of the fabric grain. Swags can be very simple and light, or have deep folds for a more formal look.

This simple box-pleated valance has pressed pleats for a tailored look.

This curtain has French-style pleats. Buttons add a punch of color at the base of each pleat.

Swags top this pleated drapery, combining two of the basic styles—pleated and swagged—in one window treatment.

Creating Pleasing Proportions and Working with Awkward Windows

When possible, window treatments look best when raised above and extended on either side of the window frame or opening. If you think about it, you are actually creating wall treatments, not window treatments! This will frame the window, allowing for more exposure of the glass for light and the view outside. Here are some other tips to create pleasing proportions and to help disguise awkward windows and flaws.

- Extend curtains on each side to make a narrow window appear larger.

- Raise the window treatment above the frame to make a short window appear taller.

- Use arched styles or large-scale hardware to balance open wall space above a window.

- When raising draperies or valances high above the frame, fill in the blank wall space with a false Roman shade to create the illusion of a taller window.

- Mount hardware at the same height on windows of differing heights in the same space to disguise the difference.

- Be aware of styles and trends; shorter valances are more common today.

- When making draperies for two-story windows, allow extra fullness and larger pleats. The taller the draperies, the skinnier they will look.

- Add interlinings to curtains to make them appear to have more fullness.

- Sketches and scale drawings are the best way to figure out proportions!

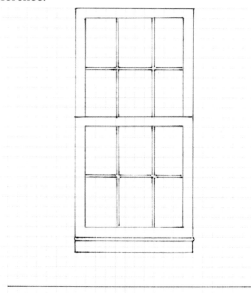

This is a sketch of a narrow window, 36 inches (91.4 cm) wide and 84 inches (213 cm) from the top of the frame to the floor. The ceiling height is 8 feet (2.4 m). The next three sketches show how different proportions can change the appearance of the same style of window treatment.

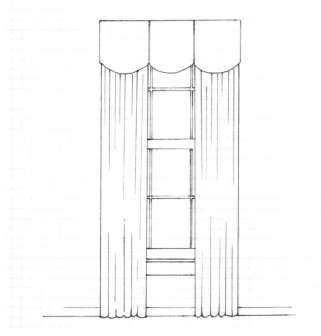

The drapery panels are extended 3 inches (7.6 cm) beyond the frame on both sides, and the top treatment is raised 3 inches (7.6 cm) above the frame. This covers a lot of the view, and makes the window look small and crowded.

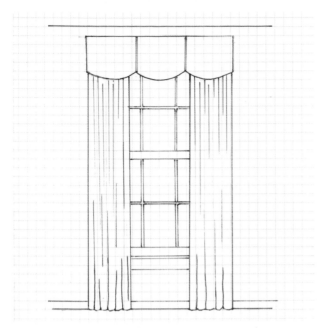

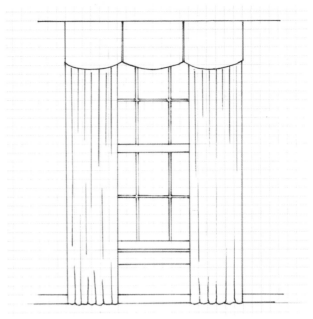

In this example, the drapery panels are extended 6 inches (15.2 cm) beyond the frame on both sides, and the top treatment is raised 6 inches (15.2 cm) above the frame. This has a more pleasing proportion and a more open view.

The window looks much larger when the drapery panels are extended 12 inches (30.5 cm) beyond the frame on both sides, and the top treatment is raised to the ceiling. This style uses the most fabric and covers the most wall space.

Understanding Use and Purpose

Window treatments play an important part in the overall room design. Before you fall in love with a style, consider the purpose of your new window treatment. This will help narrow down your choices.

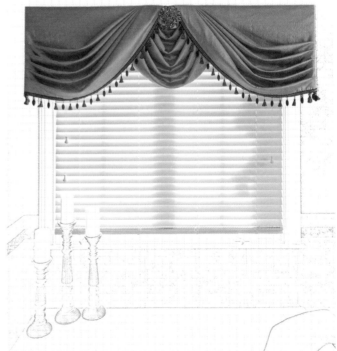

- Do you need light control?

- Do you want insulation from heat and cold?

- Would you like added privacy at the window?

- Do you want to make the window look larger or have better proportions?

- Are there small children or elderly people living in the home?

- What mood or style do you want to create for the room?

- What is the budget?

- What hardware will be needed and how will it be installed?

Answers to the above questions can help you create the best style for your room, and prevent costly mistakes and disappointments. A window treatment can be purely decorative, but it can also perform multiple jobs within one design.

An elegant swag top treatment is combined with a blind for privacy over this tub.

Measuring

Measuring your window is easy and essential to starting your project.

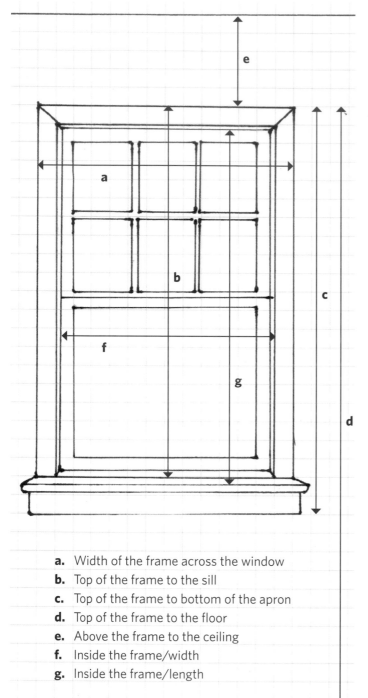

a. Width of the frame across the window
b. Top of the frame to the sill
c. Top of the frame to bottom of the apron
d. Top of the frame to the floor
e. Above the frame to the ceiling
f. Inside the frame/width
g. Inside the frame/length

An example of how to measure a typical window.

WHAT YOU WILL NEED

- good-quality, 25-foot (7.6 m) metal tape measure
- ladder or stepladder
- pencil and paper
- digital camera
- cardboard if making templates for bay window angles

While measuring, make notes about the purpose, style, and design of the finished window treatment.

Measure the window frame or opening across the width (a). If there is a wall, furniture, or some other obstruction on the side, be sure to measure the area on each side of the window. *Do you have room to extend the treatment on the left and right?*

Measure the window frame or opening from the top and down the length to the sill (b), then below the apron (c) or to the floor (d). *What length is best for the style you have selected?*

Measure above the window frame to the ceiling or crown molding (e). *Do you have space to raise the treatment above the window?*

For inside-mounted treatments, measure inside the frame or opening across the width (f) and length (g). Measure at several points, and if the sizes differ, use the lesser measurement. *Is there enough room inside for the style selected and how it will be mounted?*

While measuring, take time to plan where the hardware will be installed. *Are there obstructions like beams, cabinetry, alarm systems, speakers, or heating vents?*

Measure projections of the window frame and sill, and any existing window coverings like blinds or shutters. *How much clearance will be needed for curtains or top treatments?*

Your digital camera is an important tool. Print photos of your windows and add notes and measurements. You can make copies and sketch design ideas right on the photo!

MEASURING LARGE WINDOWS

Measuring large windows can be a challenge. It is very helpful to have another person to help you with this job. Professionals use laser-measuring devices and other tools specifically for tall and wide windows, but you can accomplish the job with a good, heavy-duty tape measure and some creativity!

Two-Story Windows

- Use a ladder for measuring. From the ladder, measure from one point up, and then from this point down, passing the tape to your helper. Add the measurements together.

- If there is a balcony or an open stairway, you can often measure from a point on the wall that is similar, such as crown molding or framing. You can stand on the balcony and measure up to the ceiling.

- Plan how you will install your finished window treatments. If possible, allow space above when deciding on a finished length so that hardware can be adjusted on-site, and a perfect length isn't necessary.

- Hiring a professional, insured installer with the right tools and experience is money well spent!

Bay Windows

Measure each window individually as shown for a standard window, plus measure the spaces between to each corner. Make a cardboard template of each angle. A protractor can also be used to determine the angles.

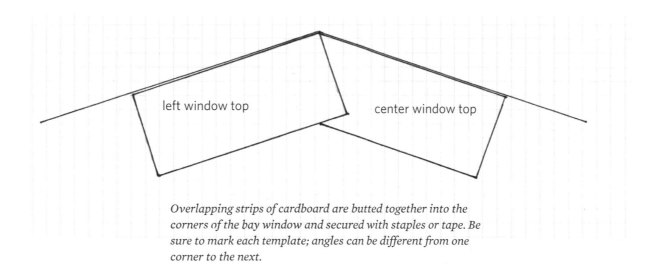

left window top

center window top

Overlapping strips of cardboard are butted together into the corners of the bay window and secured with staples or tape. Be sure to mark each template; angles can be different from one corner to the next.

Selecting Fabric

Fabrics are the reason for this book! If you love to sew and decorate, then you probably love fabric, too. Without fabrics, our windows are boring and flat. There are many different types and styles of fabrics available for window treatments.

Popular home décor fabrics include woven and printed designs.

When shopping for fabrics, select ones that are suitable for your specific project. It isn't just about color and pattern, although they are certainly big parts of the equation! Touch and feel the fabric. This is known as the "hand" of the fabric, and it will help you know how it will perform. Is it soft? Stretchy? Coarse? Does it wrinkle easily?

If it is printed, check to see if the printed design is even across, or off-grain. A defect like this could possibly be hidden in a gathered curtain, but would be a poor choice for a square and straight style like a box-pleated valance or Roman shade.

HOME DÉCOR FABRICS

The most common fabrics used in making window treatments are cotton, cotton blends, silk, linen, and polyester. Some fabrics, like "faux silk," may look like a natural fiber but they are not! Most fabrics sold for home décor are treated for stain and moisture resistance and are generally 54 inches (137 cm) wide.

Cotton fabrics are easy to work with, and will hang, drape, and wear very well. Silk is thin and lightweight, so adding extra protection and weight with interlinings is recommended.

Linen, rayon, and viscose can shrink and stretch. Linen is affected by humidity, heat, and sun. Look for linen blends for more stability.

Polyester fabrics wrinkle less, but they are difficult to dress and train into even folds for styles like pleated draperies. Upholstery-weight fabrics are generally not a good choice for window treatments, but there are exceptions.

Some styles can work up well with heavier fabrics, such as grommet draperies, Roman shades, and, of course, upholstered cornices!

Fiber Content: Natural or Manufactured

Natural fibers are plant based and include cotton, linen, and hemp, or animal based, such as wool and silk. Manufactured or synthetic fibers include polyester, nylon, and acrylic. Rayon and viscose are synthetic fibers made from an organic cellulose base. The decision whether to choose fabric made from natural or man-made fibers depends on your personal esthetic and how the window treatment will be used. Linen wrinkles and can shrink and stretch, but it can be gorgeous in the right circumstances. For outdoor use you can't beat solution-dyed acrylic fabrics.

Weave Types

Fibers are woven together to create cloth. There are many different weaving techniques used, which create different fabrics. Common weaves seen in home décor fabrics include sateen, twill, brocade, jacquard, and pile.

Fabric Styles

Once the cloth is woven, it can be printed or treated to create a specific fabric style. Chintz, for example, is a tightly woven cotton fabric that is printed and then treated to have a glossy surface. Moiré fabric is made using a calendaring process, where a ribbed fabric is forced through rollers at high heat, crushing some of the fibers to create a wavy effect. These are just two examples of how plain cloth is turned into beautiful, finished fabrics for your home.

Part of the beauty of this checked, viscose and linen blend fabric is the coarse weave.

Interlining is layered between the face fabric and the lining when making curtains.

LINING FABRICS

Linings play an important part in window treatment construction and use. The basic cotton or polyester/cotton sateen lining can be found in most window treatments that have a lining. Don't substitute another fabric for lining your curtains or shades. Linings that are manufactured and sold specifically for home décor have been preshrunk and treated for stain and moisture resistance so that they can be used at the window.

Linings help protect the face fabric from wear and sun exposure. They can also increase privacy and provide light control. Dim-out and blackout linings are used to diffuse or completely block light. Most of these linings have been manufactured with a product applied to a base cloth. For total blackout, three layers are applied to the base cloth for what is known as a "three-pass blackout." This will block light, but pinholes can be made where the needle pierces the layers applied to the fabric. This will cause pinholes of light shining through when hung at a sunny window. Substituting fusible tapes for stitching is one way to avoid this pesky problem.

Linings can also be used to keep your home warmer in the winter and cooler in the summer, especially when an interlining is layered between the face fabric and the lining. The most common interlining is cotton flannel. Flannel is a soft, napped fabric available in white and natural and in different weights. When a layer of flannel interlining is added between the main fabric and the outer lining, it creates a softer look and improves insulation.

Adding flannel interlining does not block light, but it does help diffuse light. If the main fabric is a light color, a white flannel interlining is recommended so that the light shining through the linings will not discolor the main fabric facing into the room. You can combine interlining with blackout lining for the ultimate in insulation and light control.

The heaviest of interlinings is known as "bump cloth" and adds a blanket-like layer, which is especially popular for silk draperies. Adding a layer of bump cloth creates a drapery with rounded, soft edges and deep folds. It is more sculptural and elegant and makes a statement. Another interlining similar to bump, but not as heavy, is Domette, a mid-weight twill interlining with a very soft hand.

Interlining to Create Blackout

Flannel and bump are not the only materials added in between the face and the lining fabric. Blackout lining can be used as an interlining to prevent colors from showing through to the face fabric, and it also adds structure. You will see a three-pass blackout used in soft cornices and other top treatments, and in draperies with color lining.

One of my favorite interlining techniques is the French blackout method, which layers face fabric, flannel or bump, black sateen lining, and finally the outer sateen lining in white, ivory, or khaki. This creates a blackout window treatment that is soft and luxurious. Pinholes of light are less noticeable with the French blackout because the weave of the fabrics is more forgiving than the acrylic foam coating used on typical blackout linings.

You will learn more about linings in this book, and learn how they are cut, sewn, and incorporated into the finished curtains, shades, and top treatments.

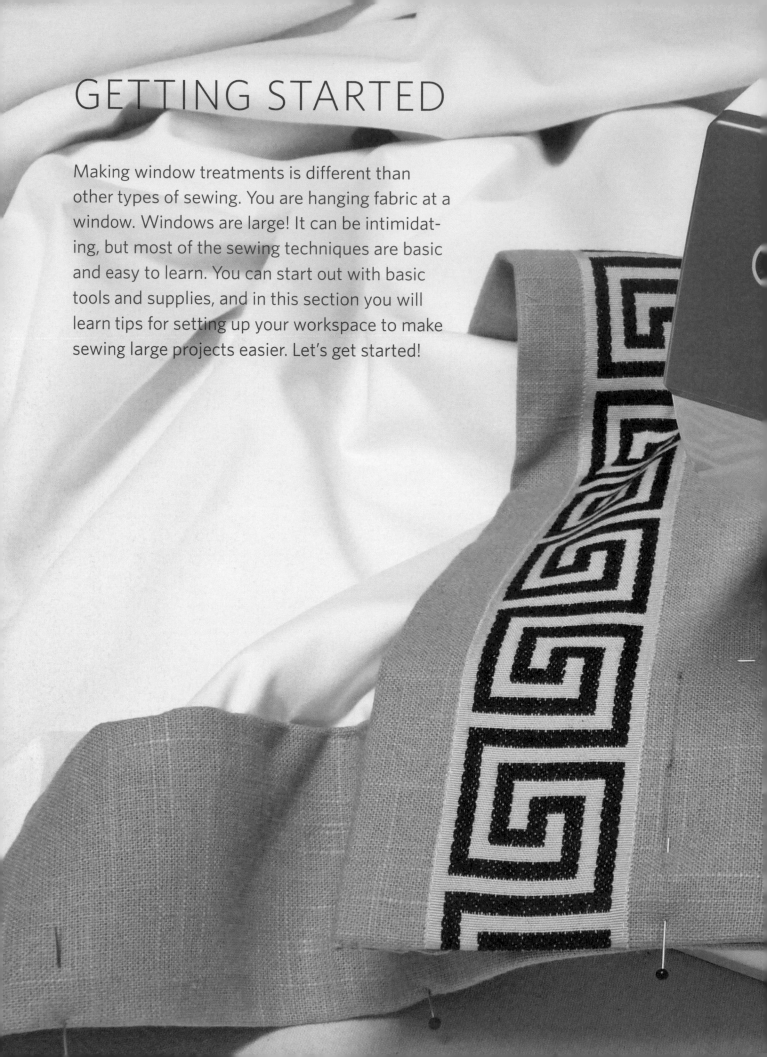

GETTING STARTED

Making window treatments is different than other types of sewing. You are hanging fabric at a window. Windows are large! It can be intimidating, but most of the sewing techniques are basic and easy to learn. You can start out with basic tools and supplies, and in this section you will learn tips for setting up your workspace to make sewing large projects easier. Let's get started!

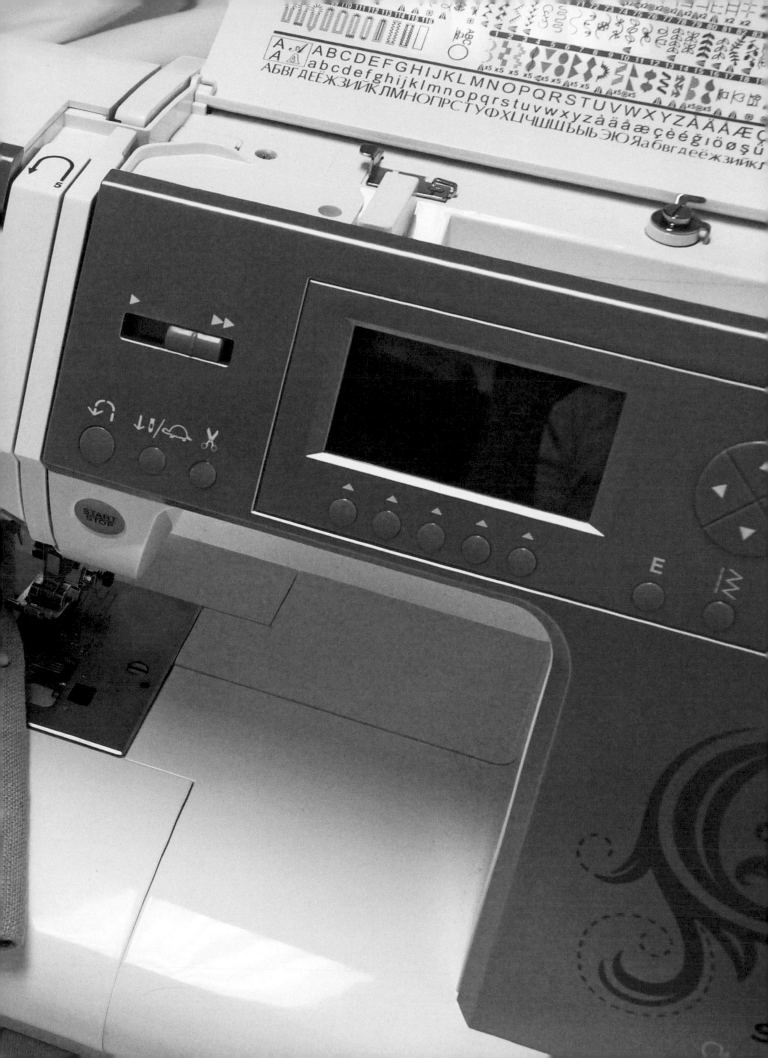

Setting Up a Workspace

Before you begin cutting and sewing, you will need to set up a functional workspace. If you do not have a sewing room, create a designated space for working on your project. Because of the size of window treatments, and the amount of fabric you will be handling, it's most helpful to have a large, sturdy worktable. In fact, it is perhaps the most important tool for making window treatments!

In a professional workroom you will find large worktables 60 inches (152 cm) wide by 10 to 12 feet (3 to 3.7 m) long. The tops are covered with canvas stretched over an underlayment for pinning and a thin layer of dense batting. This provides a large cutting and ironing surface, and fabrics can be secured by sticking pins into the underlayment.

You can make a temporary worktable with a dining or Ping-Pong table covered in foam interlocking floor tiles and a quilt, secured with tape or ties under the sides and corners. For a more permanent sewing table, cover plywood with ceiling tiles or insulation board for pinning, top with thin batting, and then stretch heavy canvas over the top, stapling it under the edges. You can place this on top of folding tables with nonskid rug pads to prevent slipping, or secure it to shelving units or even sawhorses. This is much better than trying to work on the floor.

Make sure you have adequate lighting and ventilation. If you are working in a garage or basement with concrete floors, use foam tiles or anti-fatigue mats where you will be standing.

Set up sewing machines so there is plenty of room to manipulate large pieces of fabric. Additional folding tables can help hold the weight and keep fabrics off the floor. A functional and comfortable workspace will make sewing window treatments easier and more enjoyable.

A professional workroom is set up with worktables, fabric racks, a variety of machines, and organized tools and supplies. Photo is courtesy of Frances Pusch Fine Sewing for Interiors (www.FrancesPusch.com).

Common Workroom Tools and Supplies

You can begin sewing window treatments with common, everyday sewing notions and tools. The good news is that you can get started today! As you gain experience and tackle more complex styles you will need to invest in specialty tools and supplies.

An industrial sewing machine is not required, although it certainly is helpful for sewing heavy fabrics. If your machine has a compensating foot or walking foot, you will find that to be very useful.

Review the list to become familiar with common workroom materials, tools, and supplies.

MATERIALS

- **Blackout:** A lining material that has been treated to block all light. Look for a three-pass blackout material for complete light blocking.

- **Buckram:** Traditionally a woven cotton cloth stiffened with starch (aka crinoline) but modern versions can be made from polyester or heavy paper. Used to add structure in curtain and valance headings for crisp pleats. Buckram is available in different widths and sew-on or iron-on. The most common width is 4 inches (10.2 cm).

- **Bump cloth:** A very heavy, blanket-like interlining commonly used in silk for a luxurious finish.

- **Dim out:** A light-blocking material for lining window treatments. It is often called thermal lining. This material has a suede-like surface that helps diffuse light.

- **Hook-and-loop tape:** Pressure-sensitive tape like Velcro is used to attach window treatments to boards and in other areas where the fabrics need to be removable yet securely fastened.

- **Interfacing:** A woven or nonwoven material for adding body or stabilizing fabrics.

- **Interlining:** Usually flannel but can be any fabric that is sandwiched between the face fabric and the lining.

- **Lining:** A cotton, polyester, or cotton and polyester blend fabric used to cover the reverse side of a window treatment. Look for a lining material that is specifically finished for window treatments; they will perform better than other fabrics. The most common colors of lining fabrics are white, ivory, and khaki.

- **Pleating and shirring tapes:** Sew-on tapes with cords used to make curtains and valances. When the cords are pulled, the fabric makes even pleats, tucks, or gathers. These tapes can have one, two, three, or more cords depending on the style.

- **Welt cord:** Also known as piping; a cord that is covered in fabric and used to finish seams. Welt cord can be made of soft fibers, like cotton or polyester, or firm, with cellulose for upholstery or polypropylene for outdoor use. It comes in a wide range of diameters. Micro welt cord is made with cable cord.

A variety of welt cords.

SUPPLIES

- **Bead weight:** Also called sausage weight; tiny weights that are encased inside a woven strip and added to the bottom curtains for an even weight across the entire hem. Bead weight can also be covered and used in place of welt cord in seams.

- **Fabric glue:** A wet adhesive used to secure fabrics together and to apply trims. Fabric glue will seep into the fibers and when dry creates an excellent bond.

- **Hand-sewing supplies:** Needles such as long darners are suitable for sewing hems and applying trims. Curved needles are useful for awkward areas where a regular needle will not work. Thread should be strong and stable without any stretching. Hand-quilting thread is ideal for sewing hems and trims and tacking Roman shade rings. Thimbles will make hand sewing easier. Use the type of thimble that you are most comfortable with: metal, plastic, or leather.

- **Iron-on fusing web:** A quick and easy product for joining two fabrics together temporarily before sewing, or permanently for no-sew hems.

- **Low-tack tape:** Blue painter's tape can be used to mark placement of inset trims, or as a sewing guide applied next to the presser foot on your machine.

- **Machine-sewing supplies:** Keep a variety of needles for different weights of fabric. Use general-purpose thread for most fabrics and heavy-weight thread for multiple thicknesses and upholstery-weight fabrics.

- **Markers:** Keep a good assortment of markers for different colors and weights of fabrics, and for making patterns. Chalk markers come in both solid pieces and pencil styles. Disappearing or erasable markers are good for marking Roman shade rings, seam lines on face fabrics, or other areas where a temporary mark is needed. Use pencils for marking cut lengths and permanent markers when drafting paper patterns.

- **Pin hooks:** Sharp, angled hooks that are designed specifically for hanging curtains and valances. The sharp hooks are more common and easy to adjust, but you can also find traditional sew-on hooks.

- **Pins:** Long pins are needed for the thickness of layers. Glass-head straight pins will tolerate ironing. T-pins and heavy-duty pushpins are used for holding fabrics in place for stapling.

- **Shade sewing supplies:** Shades require an assortment of supplies such as rings, ribs, and other items. See the section on shades for more specific information.

- **Tack strip:** Cardboard strip used in upholstery, stapled under fabrics to create a crisp edge.

- **Weight tape:** Square weights sewn into a wide tape. Most commonly used in hems of stage curtains and other heavy, large projects.

- **Weights:** Metal pieces that are square, round, or triangular in shape and added to hems and seams to help window treatments hang properly. Traditionally, weights are made of lead, but newer versions are made of non-lead metal compounds and are safer for the environment.

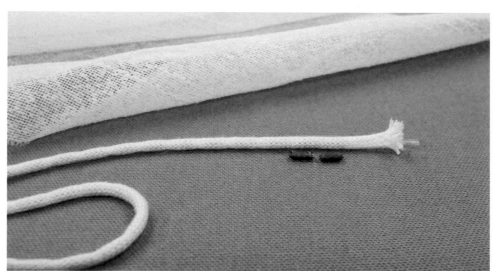

Bead weight has small pieces of weight encased in a sleeve.

TOOLS

- **Clamps:** Strong spring clamps are used to hold fabrics in place, especially when making curtains. Smaller clamps are used to hold fabrics, pleats, and bandings.

- **Cutting tools:** Good-quality scissors and shears are a great investment. Choose the size and style that best fits your hand. Long shears are good for cutting widths of fabric. Use medium-length blades for cutting around curves and shapes. Small scissors are used for cutting details and corners, and nippers are handy at the sewing machine for clipping threads. Rotary cutters can be used for cutting banding and welt cord.

- **General hand and power tools:** These are needed for making and installing window treatments. You will need a jigsaw, circular saw, heavy-duty stapler, and drill plus an assortment of screwdrivers, a tack hammer, and an awl.

- **Iron:** Use a general steam iron with a heavy sole plate. Professional workrooms will often have boiler irons, which generate steam evenly for long periods of time.

- **Measuring tools:** Every workroom has rulers in many different lengths, from short pocket-size versions to yardsticks and 48-, 60-, and 72-inch-long (122, 152, and 183 cm) rulers and a carpenter's square. A good, sturdy tape measure is a must for measuring windows and finished drapery lengths. Look for heavy-duty metal tape measures in 12- and 25-foot (3.6 and 7.3 m) lengths. A soft tape measure is used for measuring bedding, pillows, and slipcovers and to determine drops and curves. Clear quilter's rulers are wonderful for cutting bandings and welt cord, marking inset trims, and measuring hems.

- **Sewing machines:** Use a good-quality machine that can sew multiple thicknesses. The most common stitch used is a straight stitch. Occasionally a zigzag stitch is used for finishing edges or making buttonholes. An overlock machine or serger is an excellent tool for joining fabrics and finishing edges.

Workroom clamps are used to hold fabrics to the worktable, especially when making large curtains.

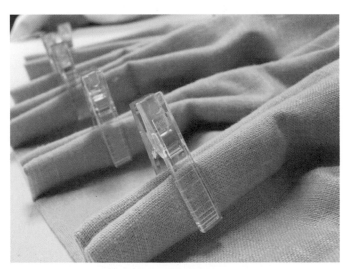

Small quilter's clamps are handy for holding fabrics.

FUNDAMENTAL TECHNIQUES

In this section you will learn the basic sewing skills that will be used over and over when making window treatments. You will learn how to cut and match pattern motifs and add hems, linings, trims, and other finishing touches. You will refer back to this section often.

Working with Fabrics

CUTTING

It is important to cut fabrics as straight and square as possible, but it can be a challenge because fabrics can shift and move. When making the initial cuts, add a few extra inches (7.6 cm) so that you will not come up short if a cut is uneven. This is called a "workroom allowance" or "tabling allowance" and is a common practice. There are several techniques for cutting, which are shared below. You will want to experiment to see what works best for the fabric at hand.

Pulling a Thread

Clip the selvage and separate one thread from the horizontal weave of the fabric and gently pull the thread to gather up the fabric.

Keep pulling until the thread breaks. Flatten out the fabric and cut along the line created by the pulled thread. When you get to the end of the line, find the end of the thread or choose another thread and keep pulling and cutting.

On some fabrics you can pull a thread and cut at the same time, holding the thread tight and keeping the blade of the scissors next to the thread. This takes a little practice but is a fast and fun way to cut fabrics square.

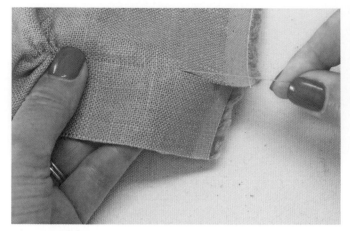

Clip the selvage and pull a thread.

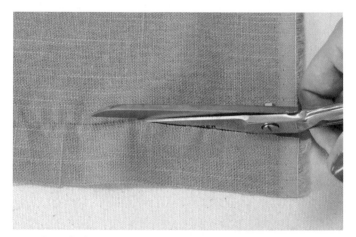

Cut along the line created by the pulled thread.

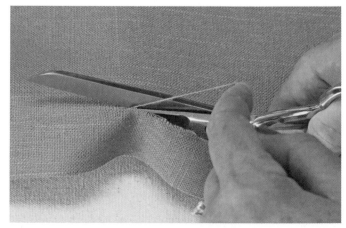

Pull a thread and hold it taut while you cut.

Folding and Cutting

Not all fabrics can be cut by pulling a thread. Another option is to fold the fabric over on itself, lining up the selvages to create a square, even fold at the cut length. Run the scissors into the fold and cut, or press a crease line as a mark. This can be an efficient way to roll out fabrics when cutting to a pattern repeat.

You can also use rulers and carpenter's squares to mark and cut fabrics. This is a good approach when fabrics are printed off-grain, so that you can work with the fabric face up and make slight adjustments if needed.

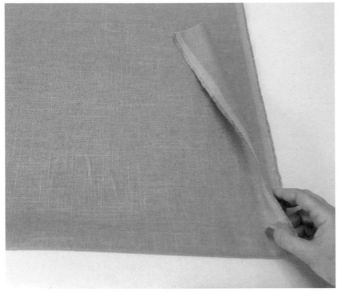

Fold the fabric so that the selvages are even on each side.

Cut along the fold.

Fold patterned fabrics to the length needed to match the pattern repeat and cut along the fold.

Join fabrics with a serged seam to prevent fraying.

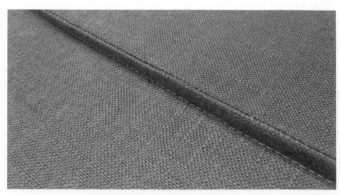

Use a French seam for unlined window treatments.

SEAMS

Fabrics are joined together with simple seams, sewn with a straight stitch. The size of the seam allowance depends on the selvage width or the pattern match. Do not cut off the selvages until you have determined how the fabric will be sewn.

After sewing, the selvages can then be trimmed to ½ inch (1.3 cm) from the stitch line. The seams can be pressed open or pressed to one side. A serged seam can be used for fabrics that fray or that will be unlined, and the seam pressed to one side.

An encased, French seam is used when the seam will be visible, such as with unlined curtains. To make a French seam, stitch or serge together the fabrics with wrong sides together. Turn the fabric along the seam with right sides together, press, and pin. Sew to the outside of the seam, encasing the seam.

HEMMING

Hems are used along the side and bottom edges, and are usually folded over twice for extra body and to hide cut edges.

Hand sewing gives the best-quality finish. Press hems and pin. Set the pins at an angle and bury the points to prevent snags and picks. For hand sewing hems, use a strong thread like one suitable for hand quilting and long, sharp needles (darners) plus a pair of nippers and a thimble.

A slipstitch, running stitch, overcast stitch, or blanket stitch can all be used to sew hems. To make the hem less visible, catch only a tiny amount of the fabric with the needle and space the stitches evenly about ½ inch (1.3 cm) apart.

A machine-sewn blind stitch can also be used. Test the fabric first to make sure it will feed evenly. You will want to set the stitches so that the least amount of stitching shows. For some projects, a straight stitch can be used to finish the hems. This is a sturdy, practical finish for curtains that will be washed. Straight stitching can also be used as a decorative detail in a contrasting color.

Fusible hemming tape can be used for a quick and easy finish. Test the fabric first to make sure the fabric can accept a hot iron, and that the tape doesn't show through to the front.

Side hems often have lining and even interlining included in the folds, which can make them thicker. They are not more difficult to sew, but the extra layers can cause take-up or puckering. Hand sewing is ideal for side hems, but they can also be finished by machine or with fusible products.

Fold a doubled hem and pin. Sew along the underside of the hem, stitching into the fold and into the lining only, and catching the face fabric about every 6 inches (15.2 cm), or a hand width apart, with a tiny stitch to the front. Keep the tension on the thread even and not too tight. You don't want dimples to show on the front! At the corners, use a ladder stitch for a neat and invisible finish.

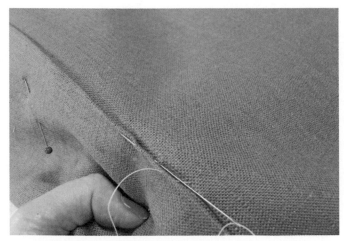

Use a slipstitch for an invisible hem from the front and back. The thread is hidden inside the fold.

Use a blanket stitch when the project is lined.

Use a blind hem attachment to finish hems by machine.

Use a ladder stitch to close bottom corners on side hems. Pull the thread so the stitches are hidden.

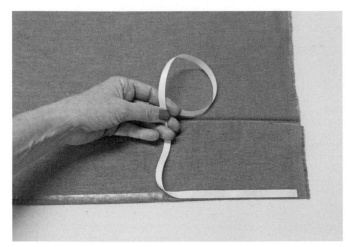

Press fusible hem tape to the top back edge of the hem fold. Fold over again and press to finish.

Hide the stitches under the edge of the hem. Sew into the lining but only catch the face fabric with a tiny stitch every 6 inches (15.2 cm).

MATCHING PATTERN MOTIFS

When working with patterned fabrics you will want to match the pattern at the seams, so the design will be consistent across the window treatment, and from one window in the room to another. Look at the fabric and find a repeating design, such as a flower, and measure.

When purchasing fabric, the pattern repeat is factored into the calculations. You will divide the cut length by the pattern repeat to determine the adjusted cut length.

For example, if you need 96-inch (244 cm) cuts for your project and the pattern repeat is 27 inches (68.6 cm), you will divide 96 by 27 for a result of 3.5. In order to have enough fabric for matching, round up to 4 repeats per cut. The adjusted cut length is 27 inches x 4 = 108 inches (274.3 cm).

There are different types of pattern repeats, from centered to offset designs. Most fabrics will have a pattern that matches straight across so that when you cut to a repeat, all the cuts will line up evenly. But there are some fabrics with a "drop repeat," where the motif does not match straight across from one selvage to the other. The pattern might drop half of a repeat, or even a whole repeat.

When using a drop repeat there will be some waste, as you adjust to match patterns. But with some planning, the waste is minimized. Plan your first cut, then drop down to make the next cut to match. If you were to make all the cuts the same, you will end up with an uneven match. When sewing multiple widths together, plan your first cuts and then the drop match cuts. For example, if you need three cuts, you will cut two exactly alike and then drop down to the matching motif and cut one more. You only waste one repeat.

Measure the pattern repeat from one flower to the next matching flower.

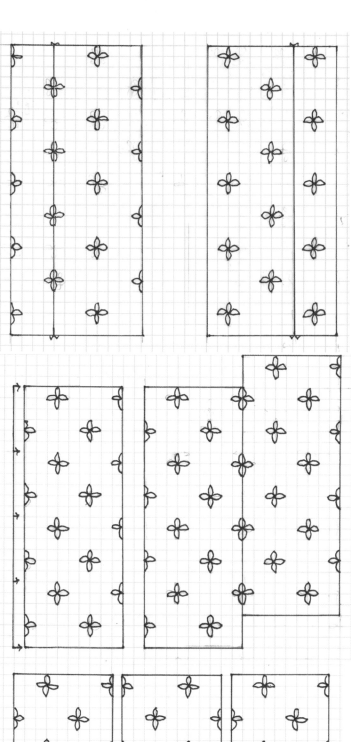

Examples of centered and offset pattern motifs matched with one and a half widths of fabric.

There are four repeats in this example of a drop repeat. You will come up short if you cut both pieces the same because the pattern doesn't line up across the width.

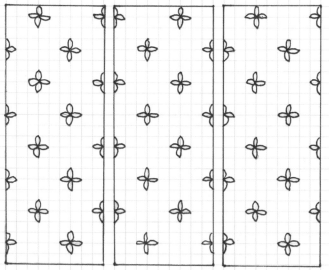

Three widths are cut to match a drop repeat with the center section using a different starting motif than the two outer cuts.

JOINING FABRICS AND MATCHING PATTERNS

After your fabric is cut, mark the direction of the pattern motif on each cut. Sometimes there will be an arrow on the selvage indicating the direction, but not all fabrics have this. You can mark with a pin at the bottom, or a piece of tape.

Two methods for matching patterns are shown using fusible tape or pins. Practice both techniques and use the best option for your project.

Matching with Fusible Tape

1. Place one piece of fabric face up. Fold under the selvage edge of the next piece of fabric to determine where the pattern will match. The match might be right at the edge of the selvage, or over into the design. (A) Once you find the match, press under the selvage so that it matches the other piece. (B)

2. Apply iron-on fusible tape along the edge, under the fold. (C) Remove the paper strip (D) and with both fabrics face up iron the fabrics together, matching the pattern and joining the fabrics with the fusible tape. (E)

3. Fold the fabrics face to face and stitch in the crease line. Cut off the excess selvage to ½ inch (1.3 cm). You can also serge the seam. Press the seam to one side.

With the fabrics face up, fold under the selvage on one piece to find where it matches.

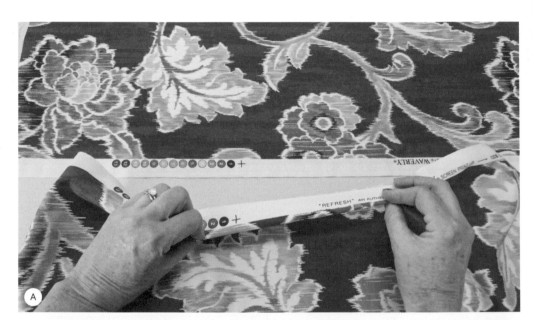

Press under the selvage to match.

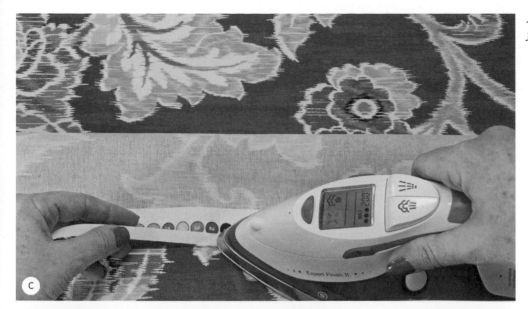

Apply fusible tape under the folded edge.

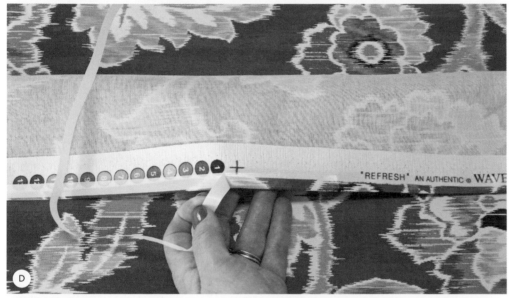

Peel away the paper strip.

Iron the fabrics together, melting the fusible tape and matching the pattern.

Matching with Pins

1. Place one piece of fabric face up and the other piece on top face down, with the patterns going in the same direction and the selvage edges lined up evenly. Fold over the selvage to find where the pattern matches and press a crease. (A)

2. Carefully stab pins through the crease, into the fabric below and back out, adding pins 3 to 4 inches (7.6 to 10.2 cm) apart. Continue down the entire edge. (B)

3. Fold the fabric over to show the crease line and stitch along the crease, removing pins as you sew. (C)

4. After the seam is sewn, cut the selvages to ½ inch (1.3 cm) and press the seams open, or press to one side, depending on your fabric and project. (D)

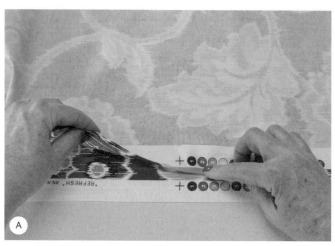

A

Fold over the selvage to find the match.

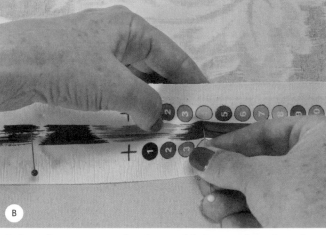

B

Pin into the crease, securing the two fabrics together where the pattern matches.

C

Stitch on the crease line.

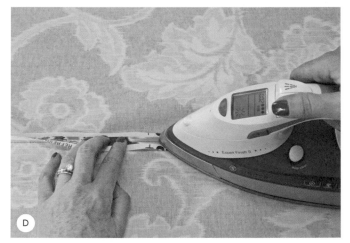

D

Press the seam open.

Frills and Trims

From fringe and ruffles to banding, braid, and decorative cord, there are many different types of trim that can be used to embellish your window treatments. You can purchase trims like fringe and braid, or make your own from fabric to add details like banding and welt cord.

There are many types of fringe to choose from. Tassel fringe has a braid with attached tassels in solid or mixed color combinations. Tassel fringe can have acrylic, metal, or wood accents. A variety of methods can be used to apply tassel fringe. The braid edging can be sewn by hand or machine or applied with fabric glue, letting the tassels hang free.

Bullion fringe is woven with a braid and long cords. It comes in a variety of sizes and in solid or combined colors. Bullion fringe is most often applied with glue or hand stitching. Look for bullion fringe along the bottom of upholstered pieces.

Brush fringe has a thick, bushy edge and is most often machine sewn in seams. When you purchase brush fringe it has a chain stitch holding all the threads together. Leave this stitching in place until all sewing is finished, and then pull the threads away and fluff up the fringe.

Gimp braid is commonly used because it is a less expensive style of trim, and it can turn curves and corners easily. Use gimp to outline shapes or as a simple detail on curtains. It is often used in upholstery to cover tacks and staples and is often glued in place.

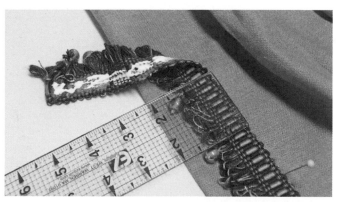

Fabric glue can be used to attach trim. Test first to make sure the fabric and trim can accept the glue without becoming discolored. Once the glue is set, the trim cannot be removed.

Hand sew fringe with a strong thread in a matching color. Hand sewing is a gentle application. The fringe can be removed without damaging the fringe or fabric.

Inset gimp braid to accent shaped edges like on this cornice board.

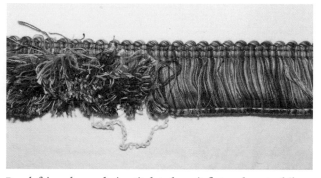

Brush fringe has a chain stitch to keep it flat and neat while sewing.

Flat banding is used on curtains and top treatments to create a more tailored look. The Greek key design is a classic pattern. Flat bandings can be machine stitched or glued in place.

Decorative cords come in many styles and diameters. The most common is twist cord, which has individual cords wound together to create one cord, in solid or variegated colors. Twist cord is available with an attached lip, which is machine sewn into the seam. You can also find twist cord without a lip that is used for tiebacks, formed into decorative knots, or as an edging along interior moldings.

Use small dots of fabric glue to hold the trim temporarily in place until it has been sewn. This prevents puckering and take-up and is faster than using pins. Low-tack blue tape marks the placement of the trim.

Sew neatly along both edges with a matching thread.

MAKING TRIMS FROM FABRIC

There are many trimming options that you can make yourself. Custom welt cord, ruffles, and banding will set your work apart.

Covered Welt Cord

Welt cord (also called piping cord) is used in seams as a decorative detail and also strengthens and adds body to seams and edges. You will see it used often on the projects in this book. Welt cord comes in many different diameters, but for window treatments the most common size is ½ inch (1.3 cm) diameter or less.

Cover welt cord with fabric that is cut into strips. Cut on the bias or diagonal of the fabric if the cord will be sewn around shapes or curves.

1. To determine the cut size, wrap the fabric around the cord, adding for the seam. The size will vary based on the thickness of the fabric and the diameter of the cord. (A)

2. Sew the strips together. Use a zipper foot or welt cord foot to sew the fabric around the welt cord. Do not sew too close to the cord. (B)

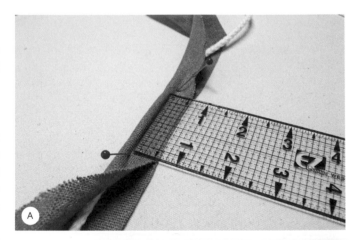

3. Sew the covered cord to the main fabric. (C)

4. Sew the front to the back, getting close to the welt cord. The last stitch line should be snug against the cord. (D)

Finished welt cord.

Ruffles

To make ruffles, cut strips of fabric two times the finished width of the ruffle plus 1 inch (2.5 cm). With wrong sides together, sew the pieces together and press the seams open. Fold in half and press. Sew or serge along the edge.

Gathered ruffles require two to two and a half times fullness. To create gathers, zigzag over a narrow, strong cord along the top edge. Tie off the cord at one end and pull the other, gathering the fabric neatly. (If you don't have cord, you can use dental floss or fishing line.) You can also make gathered ruffles by pinching the fabric under the presser foot as you sew, or by using a ruffling attachment.

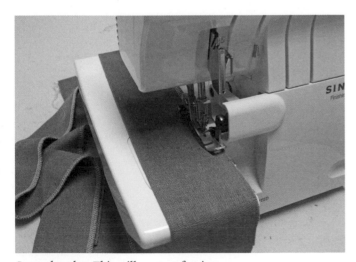

Serge the edge. This will prevent fraying.

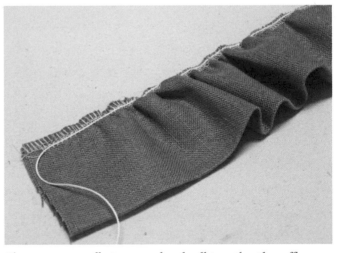

Zigzag over a small, strong cord and pull to gather the ruffle.

Pleated ruffles require at least three times fullness. To make a box-pleated ruffle, mark along the top edge as shown in the illustration. The space that is pleated is always double the box ruffle. For a 1-inch (2.5 cm) box ruffle, you will mark 1 inch (2.5 cm), 2 inches (5 cm), 1 inch (2.5 cm), 2 inches (5 cm), and so on. Fold the ruffle to create the boxes as you sew, folding forward, then backward.

To make knife-pleat or accordion ruffles, mark along the top edge double the finished size of each pleat. For a 1-inch (2.5 cm) finished pleat, you will mark 2 inches (5 cm), 2 inches (5 cm), 2 inches (5 cm), and so on. At the sewing machine, fold over to each mark and stitch.

Banding

Banding is a popular trim, and can be made in any width and inset from the edge, or applied along the edge of curtains, valances, or shades.

A small wrapped banding can be used to encase cut edges. Cut the banding strips four times the finished banding size and sew the pieces together. With the fabrics pinned together right sides out, sew the banding strip to the edge using a seam the size of the finished banding. Wrap from the front to the back, pressing the banding and turning under the cut edges. Finish the banding on the back by hand sewing or with fabric glue.

Cut the banding fabric on the bias when it will be sewn around curves. You are limited to a narrow ½- to ¾-inch (1.3 to 1.9 cm) banding when cutting on the bias.

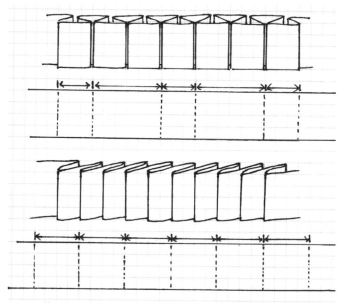

Box pleat, knife pleat, and gathered ruffles.

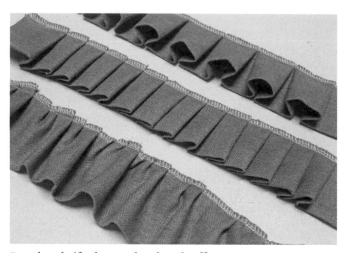

Box ruffles are pleated forward and back. Knife pleats all fold in the same direction.

Sew the banding face down to the front and turn under to the reverse.

Cut banding on the bias for curved edges like this.

For a wide shaped banding, the fabric will need to be cut to the same shape. In this example, welt cord is used between the banding and along the bottom edge. **(A)**

1. Sew welt cord to the bottom edge of the top section and press the seam allowance under to the reverse side. Cut a wide strip of the banding fabric. Place the valance with cording attached face up over the fabric strip. (For this valance, the pieces are interlined.) **(B)**

2. Glue under the edge to hold it in place. When the glue is dry, turn the fabric back and sew next to the welt cord. **(C)**

3. Trim away excess fabric where the cording is sewn and press the pieces from the front.

4. Glue a second piece of welt cord following the shape, using a small amount of glue under the seam allowance. **(D)** Set the cording the distance of the finished banding. **(E)**

5. After the bottom row of cording is attached, place the valance face down on the lining fabric, which is face up. Pin and sew next to the welt cord. Cut off excess fabric, turn right sides out, and press. **(F)**

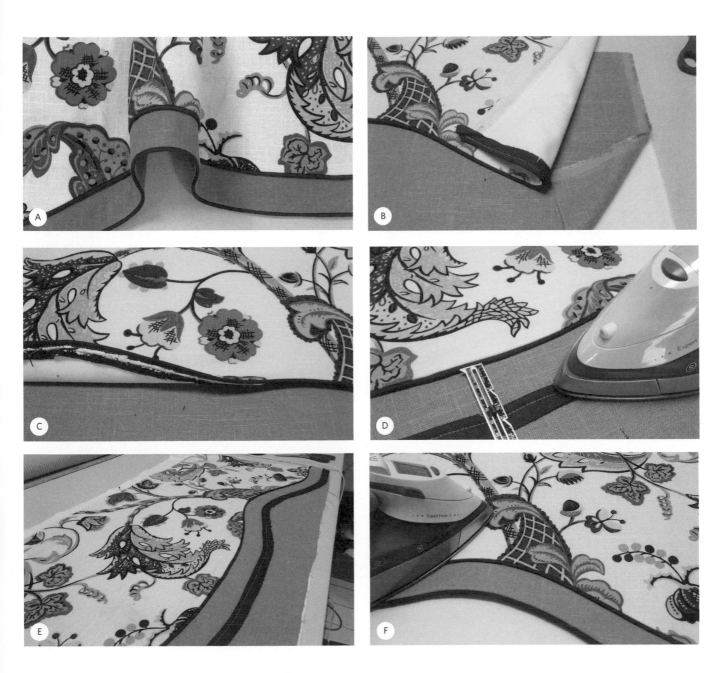

Shaped, inset banding is made by wrapping fabric around a piece of iron-on interfacing cut to the finished shape. For curtains and valances, use a light- to medium-weight interfacing. A heavy interfacing or buckram can be used for cornice boards.

1. Draw the finished banding shape on fusible interfacing and cut out. Iron the shaped piece to the back of the banding fabric. For large projects, the fabric may need to be seamed together. Overlap the interfacing slightly if it is cut in pieces. **(A)**

2. Clip around curves and corners, turning and pressing the edges over the interfacing. Glue the cut edges to the back. **(B)**

Cut fusible interfacing to the finished shape and apply to the back of the banding fabric. Cut around the interfacing, leaving a ½-inch (1.3 cm) seam allowance on the top and bottom edges.

Clip the edges, fold over, and glue to the back.

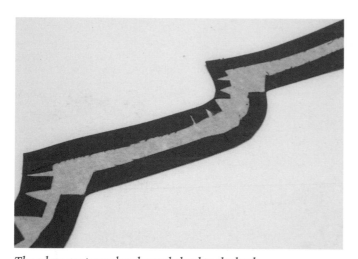

The edges are turned under and glued to the back.

Glue or sew the banding to the main fabric. See the finished project in Chapter 6: Top Treatments, beginning on page 143.

For straight banding, you may need to create a miter for right angles.

1. Cut the banding twice the finished width and press the cut edges under, to the center. **(A)**

2. Place the banding face up and inset from the edge. At the corner, turn at a right angle, measuring to make sure it is accurate and square. Fold under the corner to create a mitered fold. **(B)** Press and pin in place. **(C)**

3. The banding can be machine or hand sewn. If topstitching, use a matching thread and sew carefully so that the banding doesn't shift or pucker. You may want to baste the banding with fabric glue under the edges before sewing. **(D)**

4. If hand sewing, the miter can be flattened under the corner **(E)** and sewn with a ladder stitch. **(F)**

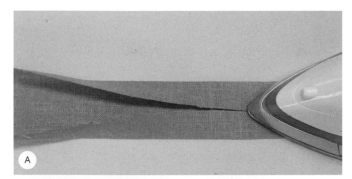

Press the edges together on the back.

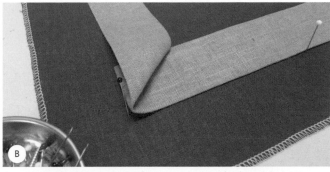

Turn the corner at a right angle, creating a mitered fold.

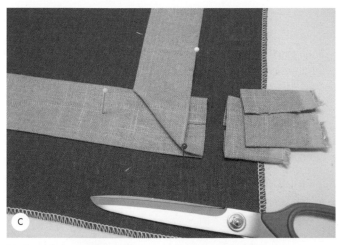

Tuck under cut edges where two pieces are joined.

Topstitched inset banding.

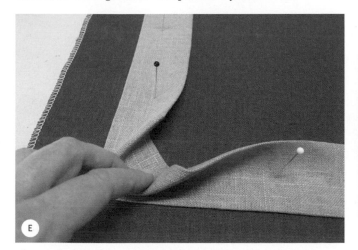

Flatten the banding under the mitered corner if hand stitching.

Use a ladder stitch to sew the mitered corner.

Overlap the banding pieces.

Glue under the mitered fold.

Unfold the banding and pin along the creases.

When the banding is ***along the edge***, like on a Roman shade, the fabric will wrap from the front to the back. The mitered corner is sewn on the inside before the banding is applied.

1. Cut the banding strips four times the finished width. Press the cut edges to the center, then fold over and press again. Place the banding pieces straight and at a right angle, overlapping the ends. Leave excess past the end for seam allowances. **(A)**

2. Fold one piece of banding on top of the other, creating a miter fold at the corner. Add fabric glue under the mitered fold only and press to set. **(B)**

3. After the glue is dry, carefully unfold the banding. You will see creases in an M shape. Pin well. **(C)**

4. Sew, carefully following the crease line using a short stitch length. After the banding is sewn, cut off excess fabric ¼ inch (6 mm) from the seam. **(D)**

5. The banding is ready to apply to the edges. Place the lining fabric face down and top with the main fabric, face up. Place the banding face down around the edges and pin well. Sew in the first crease, inset from the edge. **(E)**

6. After the banding is sewn, press from the front **(F)**, then fold under the banding to the back, pressing the edges and covering the stitch line. **(G)** Finish the banding by hand sewing, or with fabric glue or fusible tape.

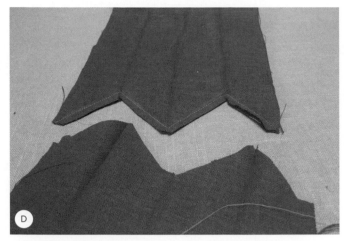

Trim off excess fabric ¼ inch (6 mm) from the seam.

Pin the banding to the edges for sewing.

Press the seam from the front before folding the banding to the reverse.

Press the banding from the back, making sure it covers the stitch line.

A Roman shade trimmed with banding.

Understanding Fullness

The term *fullness* describes the amount of extra fabric needed to create pleats or gathers in fabric in relation to the finished size. A common fullness ratio used in window treatments is to multiple two and a half times the rod, window, or finished width.

As you study the instructions, you will see the recommended fullness for different styles. Some window treatments require very little to no fullness. A flat, Roman shade doesn't require any fullness. The only extra fabric used is an allowance for hems. This style uses less fabric than a gathered or pleated shade.

In the illustration below, you can see the difference between two, two and a half, and three times fullness. Two times fullness is used for flat panel styles like grommet or tab-top curtains, two and a half times fullness gathers nicely for rod pocket or shirred and pleated curtains, and three times fullness is used for very generous, full pleated curtains.

The more fullness you use, the more fabric you will need. When calculating yardage you may choose to go down to the lesser fullness to save fabric, or move up to the greater fullness if the windows arc tall or more fabric is needed to achieve the desired results.

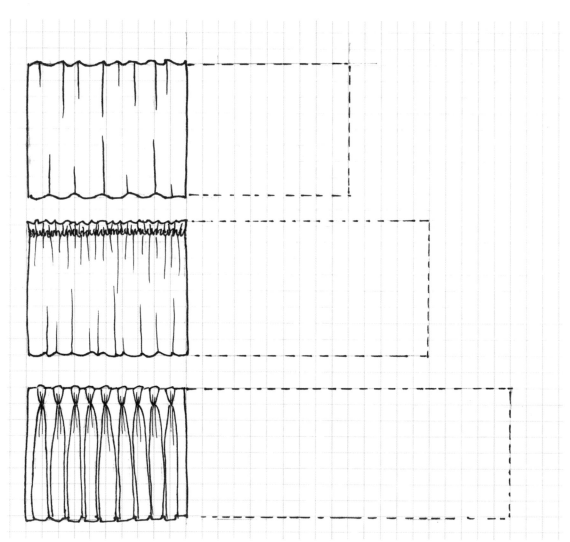

Examples of fullness.

Cord Safety

Cords on window treatments like curtains, shades, and blinds can pose a potential strangulation hazard to young children. According to the U.S. Consumer Product Safety Commission, corded window coverings are among the top five hidden hazards in American homes. This is especially important with older window coverings that may not meet the latest national standards for window cord safety.

Why Are Cords Dangerous?

Children can become entangled in operating cords dangling on the side or front of the window covering and cords on the back of shades can be pulled away from the fabric, creating a loop.

Safety Products and Standards

In the United States and other countries, safety standards are now in place for manufacturers, importers, and retailers to follow. The standards are created by a collaboration of industry organizations, government agencies, and consumer groups. Since the implementation of safety standards, there has been an increased awareness of cord safety and exciting, new product innovations.

On styles with vertical lift cords like Roman shades, cord shrouds and locks are used to control the distance that the cords can be pulled away from the window covering, lessening the size of the hazardous loop. Tension devices are used for operating systems that lift or traverse with a bead chain or cord loop, keeping it taut and anchored to the wall.

When installing new window treatments, be sure to follow the manufacturer's instructions and use the safety features and devices.

Window covering retailers, professional designers, decorators, workrooms, and window treatment installers should stay informed of new products and changes to national standards and educate clients about cord safety.

A tension device anchors the cord loop securely to the wall.

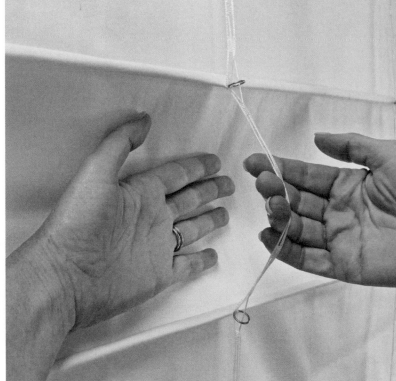

A cord shroud controls the size of the loop formed by the combination of cord and shade fabric. The shroud must be attached to the shade so that the loop stays within safety standards.

Safety Comes First, Decorating Second

It is always best practice to use cord-free window coverings. If you have old, outdated window coverings with cords, you should remove them or see if you can make them cord-free. Cords can be cut off and removed from traverse curtain rods and then easily operated by hand or with a baton. Soft shades can be retrofitted with cord shrouds, or simply set in a fixed position and the cords removed. Another practical step to ensure safety is to move all cribs, beds, furniture, or toys away from windows and window coverings.

Examples of safe, cord-free window coverings

- Grommet or tab-top curtains

- Shutters

- Pleated curtains with cord-free hardware

- Curtains gathered on a rod

- Spring roller shades

- Top treatments like gathered valances, cornice boards, or swags

- Shades and blinds with hand-lift options and no exposed cords

- Stationary, non-operable soft shades

To retrofit a traverse rod, remove the cords and attach a baton to the master carrier.

Use the baton to open and close the curtains.

A decorative valance over shutters creates a beautiful and cord-free window covering.

LEARN MORE

United States

Consumer Products Safety Commission, www.cpsc.org

Window Covering Manufacturers Association, www.wcmanet.org

Window Covering Safety Council, www.windowcoverings.org

Canada

Canada Safety Council, www.canadasafetycouncil.org

United Kingdom

The Royal Society for the Prevention of Accidents, www.rospa.com

CURTAINS AND DRAPERIES

Can you imagine a world without curtains?
They are one of the most popular styles of window
treatments and also can serve as room dividers,
backdrops, and privacy curtains. Add interlining
and your curtains will insulate your windows, and
with blackout linings you can control light. From
sheer, short café curtains to long, luxurious silk
ball gown style, every window in any room can be
complemented with curtains and draperies.

Making a Basic Curtain Panel

All curtains are made in a similar way, with hems on the bottom, sides, and top. The top hem, also known as the "heading," is then finished to create a variety of styles. A gathered curtain may have a rod pocket or a gathering tape sewn at the top, while a pleated curtain has crisp buckram added to the heading.

Multiple widths of material are sewn together to achieve the fullness needed. When possible, try to line up the seams in the face fabric and linings to prevent shadowing when light shines through the fabric.

The term *panel* is used to describe any size curtain, from a single width to multiple widths. You can have one three-width panel, for example.

Basic steps are shown here so that they do not need to be repeated for other projects in this chapter. Once you know the basic steps, you are ready to make almost any style of curtain!

Getting Started

Allow extra for the bottom hem and heading. The most common bottom hem size is 4 inches (10.2 cm) doubled (allow 8 inches [20.3 cm]). You can vary the hem size based on the project. Short curtains can have smaller doubled hems and extra-tall curtains can have larger hems.

Finished length + hem and heading allowance = cut length

What You Will Need

- decorator fabric
- lining (and interlining)
- drapery weights

Yardage Requirements

You will need to determine how much fullness your project requires to determine yardage requirements. Refer to specific projects for detailed calculations.

Making a Basic Curtain with Lining

1. Cut and prepare fabrics, joining widths if needed. Hem the bottom edge of the face fabric with a 4-inch (10.2 cm) doubled hem and for the lining use a 3-inch (7.6 cm) doubled hem. Secure a drapery weight at seams (see Chapter 2: Getting Started). Finish hems using your preferred method. (See Chapter 3: Fundamental Techniques.)

2. Place the hemmed face fabric face down, and cut off the selvage edges. Place the lining face up over the back of the hemmed fabric, smoothing it out neatly and evenly with the bottom edge inset 1 inch (2.5 cm) along the bottom hemmed edge of the face fabric. (A) If multiple widths are sewn together, line up the face fabric and lining seams, if possible.

3. Cut the lining 3 inches (7.6 cm) less than the fabric along each side. Fold over 3 inches (7.6 cm) along the side, tucking the cut edge under to create a 1½-inch (3.8 cm) doubled side hem. Press lightly. (B) Add a drapery weight inside the fold of the hem at the bottom corners. (See Chapter 2: Getting Started.) Secure with pins. (C) Repeat for the other side. When using multiple widths, pin together the fabrics down the seams and across the top before moving over to continue making the curtain.

4. Finish the side hems by hand or machine sewing.

5. Measure from the bottom to the top, marking for the finished length, allowing extra fabric to finish the top as needed for the style you are making.

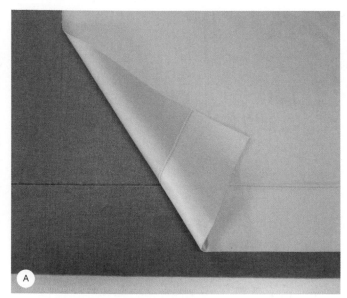

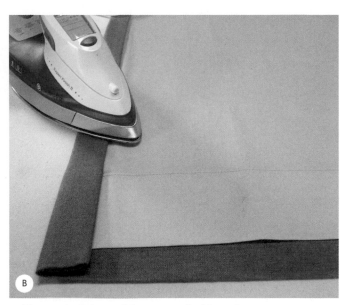

Place the lining face up over the back of the curtain panel and inset 1 inch (2.5 cm) from the bottom. Trim away excess lining even with the side edges and tuck the cut edge under the side hem.

Fold a 1½-inch (3.8 cm) hem on each side and press.

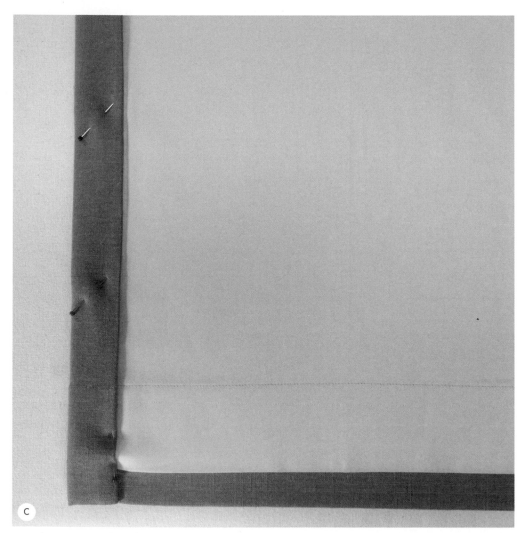

Use pins to secure the side hems.

MAKING A BASIC CURTAIN WITH LINING AND INTERLINING

1. Cut and prepare the fabrics, joining widths if needed. Hem the bottom edge of the face fabric with a 4-inch (10.2 cm) doubled hem, and for the lining use a 3-inch (7.6 cm) doubled hem. Finish the hems using your preferred method. (See Chapter 3: Fundamental Techniques.)

2. Finish the bottom edge of the interlining by serging or with a zigzag stitch.

3. Place the hemmed face fabric face down, and cut off the selvage edges. Place the interlining face up over the back of the hemmed fabric, smoothing it out neatly and evenly with the bottom edge inset 2 inches (5 cm) along the bottom hemmed edge of the face fabric. If multiple widths are sewn together, line up the face fabric and interlining seams, if possible. Cut the interlining 1½ inches (3.8 cm) less than the fabric along each side.

4. Place the hemmed lining fabric face up over the interlining with the bottom hem inset 1 inch (2.5 cm) along the bottom edge of the face fabric. Cut the lining 3 inches (7.6 cm) less than the fabric along each side. (A)

5. Fold over the face fabric along the sides to create a 1½-inch (3.8 cm) doubled hem, including the interlining in the fold and tucking the cut edge of the lining under the doubled side hem. Press lightly. Add a drapery weight to the bottom corners and at the seams. (See Chapter 2: Getting Started.) Secure with pins. (B)

6. Finish the side hems by hand or machine sewing.

7. Measure from the bottom to the top, marking for the finished length, allowing extra fabric to finish the top as needed for the style you are making. (C)

A

Along the sides of the curtain cut the interlining 1½ inches (3.8 cm) less than the face fabric, and the lining 3 inches (7.6 cm) less. When the side hem is folded over, the interlining will be included for a single fold.

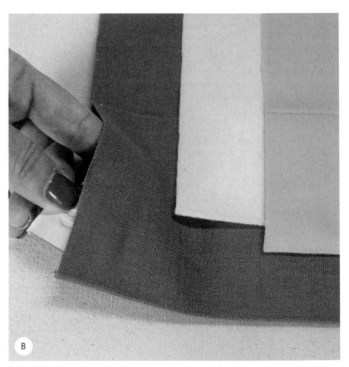

B

A drapery weight is tucked into the bottom of the side hem. Drapery weights are also added at the seams.

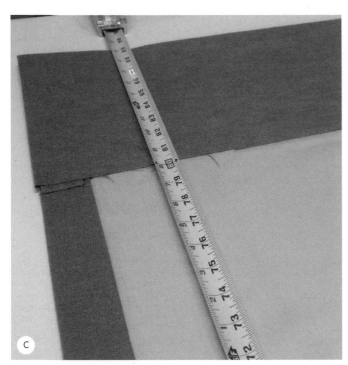

Measure from the bottom to the top, folding over at the finished length.

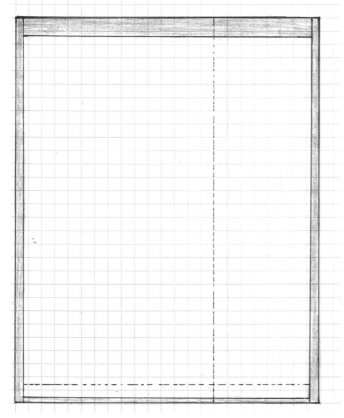

A typical curtain panel has a bottom hem, side hems, and a top heading. Vertical seams are lined up to prevent shadowing in sunlight.

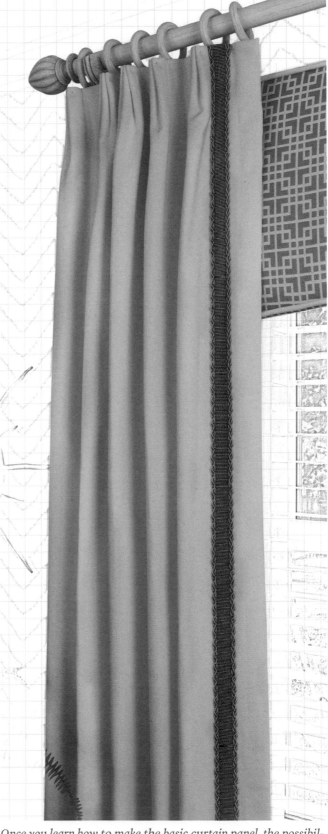

Once you learn how to make the basic curtain panel, the possibilities are endless! This pretty drapery has a pleated heading and inset trim.

Flat Curtain Styles

Flat curtain styles are more tailored and, because they use minimal fullness, require less fabric than gathered or pleated styles. But they are not boring or plain! Flat curtain styles can be very stylish, functional, and a complement to most any window.

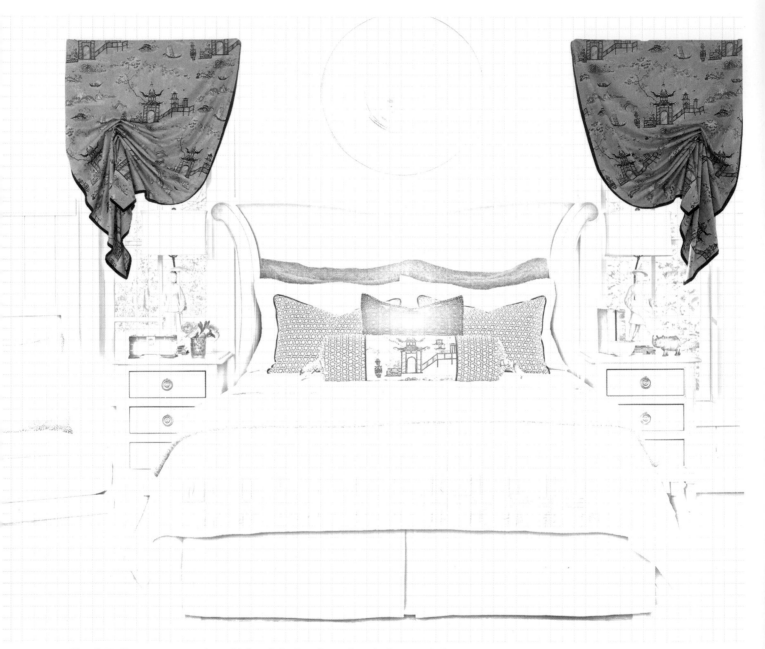

Simple Italian strung curtains with banded edges dress these bedroom windows.

ITALIAN STRUNG CURTAIN

This curtain style is incredibly easy to make, and because it is a flat style, it requires a minimal amount of fabric. The swag and tail design is created with cords and rings, lifting the panel up and to the side. This style can also be slightly pleated or gathered across the top for an even softer look.

Getting Started

For this project, a bold toile print was used for the face fabric, black sateen for the banding, and white sateen for the lining. If making unlined Italian strung curtains, finish the side and bottom edges with a small hem.

Plan to mount the board above the window frame and 1 inch (2.5 cm) beyond the frame on the sides.

For this project one Italian strung curtain was used on each window, creating a mirror-image design. For a larger width window, two curtains can be used.

What You Will Need

- decorator fabric
- lining
- mounting board cut to size
- heavy-duty stapler and staples
- tools and hardware for installation
- screw eyes
- sew-on Roman shade rings
- Safe-T-Shade RingLocks or cord shroud
- shade cord
- cord-adjusting orb

Yardage Requirements

If using a print fabric, additional fabric may be needed to match the pattern motif.

The fabric and lining are cut exactly the same. To determine the cut width, measure across the mounting board and around each end. This is the finished width of the curtain.

For the cut length, determine where you would like the longest point to fall after the curtain is drawn up and add 18 inches (45.7 cm); this is adjustable after the curtain is installed.

For the ½-inch (1.3 cm) edge banding, cut enough 2-inch (5 cm)-wide strips to finish across the bottom and down both sides of the curtain.

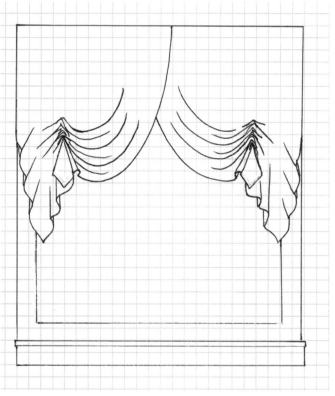

Two Italian strung curtains can be mounted to one board. This is a good choice for wider windows that require more than one width of fabric, and allows for a larger center view. Overlapping the curtains in the center will help cover the mounting board and window trim.

Making an Italian Strung Curtain

1. Cut the fabrics. Place the lining face down and top with the decorator fabric face up, lining up the edges evenly. Pin around all four sides, securing the lining and face fabric together. Sew together banding strips and press the seams open. Sew the banding strips face down along the side and bottom edges using a ½-inch (1.3 cm) seam allowance. After the banding is sewn, wrap to the reverse side, folding under the cut edges. Press neatly and pin. Finish the banding by hand sewing. (See Chapter 3: Fundamental Techniques.)

2. After the banding is complete, press the curtain and smooth it out on the work surface lining side up. Measure and mark the finished length (include an allowance for board mounting) and cut away any excess fabric. Add pins across the top to hold the layers together.

3. Measure and mark for the first ring at the bottom corner on the leading edge, inset 12 inches (30.5 cm) from side and bottom. At the top, measure 12 inches (30.5 cm) from the return edge and place a pin to mark the spot. Place a long ruler or other straight edge from the bottom mark to the top mark. Place a piece of cord below the straight edge, bowed down 6 inches (15.2 cm) at the center point and back. This is the path the rings will follow. (A)

4. Starting at the bottom point, measure along the cord and mark every 6 inches (15.2 cm) until you are within 12 inches (15.2 cm) of the top. Pin at each mark to hold the fabrics together. Sew a shade ring to each mark, making sure you catch the face fabric with the stitches.

5. Cover the mounting board and attach the curtain to the top of the board, wrapping around each end. (See Chapter 7: Installing Window Treatments.) Attach small screw eyes under the board and in line with the top ring and at the back edge. Thread cord through the rings using Safe-T-Shade RingLocks or a cord shroud. (See Cord Safety, page 45.) (B)

6. Install the curtain to the wall using angle irons. (See Chapter 7: Installing Window Treatments.) Pull the cord to raise the curtain to the desired height and secure the cord by tying off to the screw eye, or use a cord-adjusting orb. (C) Cut away excess cord and dress the curtain with even, swag-like folds. (D)

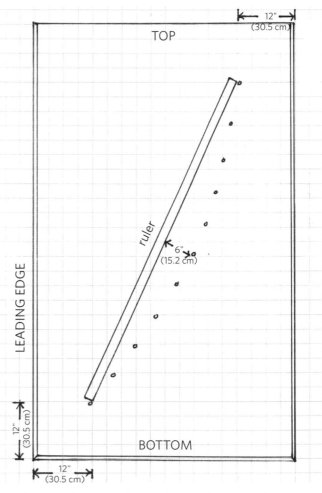

A cord is used to mark the arc for the ring placement.

Starting at the bottom point, mark along the arc for the rings every 6 inches (15.2 cm) and sew a ring to each mark.

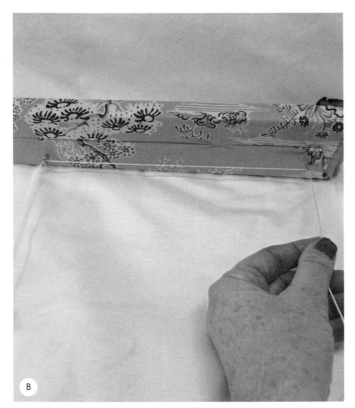

Screw eyes are attached to the board. The cord is threaded through the screw eyes and out the side.

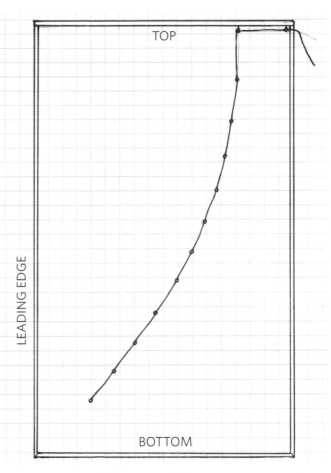

A view of the back of the curtain with rings, screw eyes, and cord.

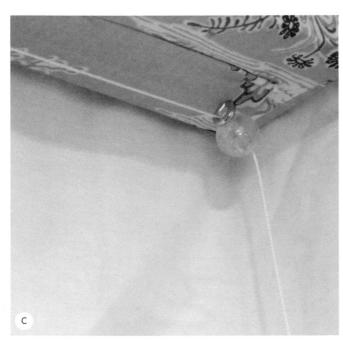

C

After raising the curtain to the desired height, a cord-adjusting orb holds the curtain in a fixed position.

D

Dress the curtain with even folds, pulling the spaces between the rings forward.

The vertical folds of this grommet curtain balance the horizontal lines of the windows and blinds. Ceiling-mounted hardware is a handsome feature and a clever solution.

GROMMET CURTAIN

Grommet curtains are a popular yet uncomplicated style. The curtain panels are flat, but when a decorative pole is threaded through the grommets, a clean, serpentine shape is formed. Because very little sewing is required, this style is a good choice for less experienced curtain makers.

Getting Started

Follow instructions for making a basic curtain. For the top heading, allow enough fabric for a double fold to the back. The amount can vary based on the diameter of the grommets. Generally, allow at least 1 inch (2.5 cm) above and below the inside edge of the grommets for the heading. For this project, a 4-inch (10.2 cm) double-fold heading was used.

Select a rod that is a smaller diameter than the grommets, so the curtain will slide easily. Plan to use grommets with an inside diameter of 30 to 40 percent more than the rod diameter if the curtain will be operable.

If possible, install the rod above the window and measure the finished width and length. Remember that the top of the rod is not the finished length—it is where the inside of the grommet sits on the rod. The top edge of the curtain will be above the rod. This is also important to remember if you are mounting close to the ceiling. Be sure to leave enough space above the rod for the top of the curtain.

Always plan for an even number of grommets so that the outside and inside edges both face in the same direction and toward the wall.

Measure the distance from the wall to the center of the pole. This is the "return." Measure the return at each end and in the center of the rod, because the window trim may jut out, making the center returns less than the outer returns.

What You Will Need

- decorator fabric

- lining

- grommets

- buckram (iron-on)

- drapery weights

- hardware for installation

Yardage Requirements

If using a print fabric, additional fabric may be needed to match the pattern motif.

FACE FABRIC

Finished length + 16 inches (40.6 cm) for the bottom hem and top heading = cut length

Finished width x 2 fullness ÷ fabric width = number of widths per window (round up)

Cut length x number of widths ÷ 36 inches (91.4 cm) = number of yards (meters) needed

LINING

Finished length + 6 inches (15.2 cm) bottom hem = cut length

Cut length x number of widths ÷ 36 inches (91.4 cm) = number of yards (meters) needed

Making a Grommet Curtain

1. Follow instructions for making a basic curtain, measuring the length and turning over excess fabric at the top. For example, allow 8 inches (20.3 cm) extra for a 4-inch (10.2 cm) double-fold heading. Iron a crease to mark the finished length. Trim away excess lining even with the finished length.

2. Turn the curtain panel so that the heading is facing you, lining side up. Cut a piece of buckram 6 inches (15.2 cm) wider than the finished panel width. Press a double fold in the top heading and place the buckram inside the fold, folding over the excess on each end (this provides more body at each end).

3. Secure the heading by using fusible hem tape or fabric glue under the folded edge.

The curtain heading is folded and pressed. Buckram is used to add stability and create a crisp, top edge.

The heading is pressed. Fusible hem tape provides a temporary hold until the grommets are set.

A

Pins mark the inside and outside returns. The measurement between the marks is then divided by seven for this one-width panel, which will have eight grommets.

B

Center a grommet over each mark and draw around the inside diameter.

4. Mark for the grommets. Begin by adding a mark for the outside return and the inside return. Measure between the marks and divide by an odd number. Generally, the grommets should be around 6 inches (15.2 cm) or less apart. (Do not space the grommets too far apart or the sections that fold behind the rod will not clear the wall.) **(A)**

5. Center a grommet over each mark and draw around the inside circumference of the grommet. **(B)**

6. Separate the grommets into two pieces, front and back. **(C)**

7. Staple in the center of each circle. Cut one hole at a time. Cut slightly larger than the mark so the grommet will not be too snug. **(D)**

8. Place the front piece of the grommet through the hole and snap the pieces together. (If using metal grommets, a setting tool will need to be used.) Continue cutting holes and setting grommets across the heading. **(E)**

9. When all the grommets are set, the curtain is ready to install. Thread the rod through the grommets with the outside and inside edges turned toward the back. **(F)**

Note: When making multiple-width panels, it is important to place the seams in the spaces that go behind the rod. To do this, make a template of the grommet placement first, before cutting and joining fabrics. Mark for seams on the template and then use this to lay out your fabrics. You may need to trim away fabric off the leading edge or slightly adjust the grommet spacing.

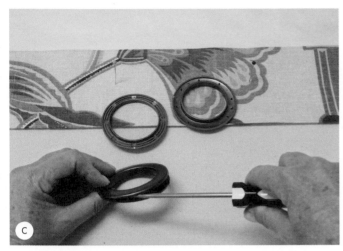

Pry apart plastic grommets with a flat screwdriver.

A staple is used in the center of each circle. This holds the heading together and makes cleanup easy!

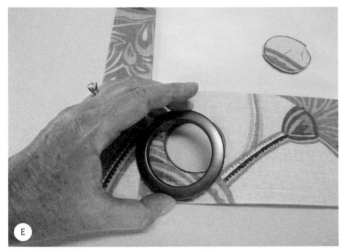

Snap together the front and back pieces of the grommet set. Glue can be added around the neck of the grommet for a more secure bond.

The finished grommet panel is ready to be installed on the window.

The grommet curtain is installed on a smooth iron rod and opens and closes easily.

WAVE CURTAIN WITH CLIP-ON RINGS

This style of curtain has a wave or serpentine shape, minimal fullness, and a clean and uncluttered appearance. The look is similar to grommet curtains, but this version is installed with clip-on rings. Vertical stitching is used to hold the layers together, and provides a hidden spot for the clip-on rings.

Getting Started

Buckram is used to hold the shape across the top. Just about any type of fabric is suitable for this style. If using a thin fabric, interlining can be added for extra body.

The wave curtain has a sleek, contemporary style.

What You Will Need

- decorator fabric
- lining
- iron-on buckram
- drapery weights
- rings with attached clips and other hardware for installation

Yardage Requirements

If using a print fabric, additional fabric may be needed to match the pattern motif.

FACE FABRIC

Finished length + 12 inches (30.5 cm) = cut length

Finished width x 2 fullness ÷ fabric width = number of widths per window (round up)

Cut length x number of widths ÷ 36 inches (91.4 cm) = number of yards (meters) needed

LINING

Finished length + 9 inches (22.9 cm) top and bottom hem = cut length

Cut length x number of widths ÷ 36 inches (91.4 cm) = number of yards (meters) needed

Making a Wave Curtain with Clip-On Rings

1. Follow instructions for making a basic curtain, adding lining and drapery weights at the side hems and seams. Measure from the bottom edge to the top, adding 4 inches (10.2 cm) to the finished length. Mark and cut off any excess fabric.

2. Turn the curtain panel so that the heading is facing you, lining side up. Cut a piece of iron-on buckram 7 inches (17.8 cm) wider than the finished panel width. Iron the buckram to the back of the fabric, even with the top edge and folding over 3½ inches (8.9 cm) of extra buckram at each end. (A)

3. Fold over and press the fabric with the buckram attached, so that the top edge of the buckram is even with the finished length. (B)

Attach iron-on buckram to the back top edge.

Fold over the buckram and fabric and press.

4. Fold under the lining across the reverse side of the curtain and, using one of the rings with clips attached, measure the distance between the ring and where it clips to the lining. For this curtain the lining will need to be 1 inch (2.5 cm) less than the top edge of the curtain to hide the clips. (C)

5. Press the lining evenly across the top. Unfold and cut off excess fabric past the crease so that it will be even with the bottom edge of the buckram that is at the top of the curtain. On this curtain, 3 inches (7.6 cm) of lining is folded under at the top, to line up evenly with the 4-inch (10.2 cm) buckram, leaving a 1-inch (2.5 cm) reveal of face fabric across the reverse side.

6. Fold and press the side hems. Sew around the corners, and finish the side hems. The curtain is ready to be marked and tacked.

7. Measure and mark for the placement of the clip-on rings. To create a return to the wall, begin with your first mark based on the size of the return on your hardware. For the leading edge, mark next to the side hem. Measure in between the two marks to create spacing that is 5 to 6 inches (12.5 to 15.2 cm) apart. (D)

8. At each mark, draw two vertical lines ¾ inch (1.8 cm) apart and ¾ inch (1.8 cm) high on the back of the lining, using an erasable or disappearing marker. This will be where each ring will be clipped.

9. Pin together the layers of fabric and buckram between the marks to hold the lining in place. (E)

10. Use iron-on fusing web to attach the lining to the back of the curtain between the marks. (F)

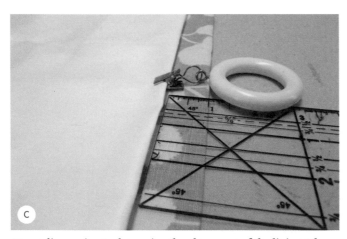

Use a clip-on ring to determine the placement of the lining. The clip will be hidden behind the top of the curtain.

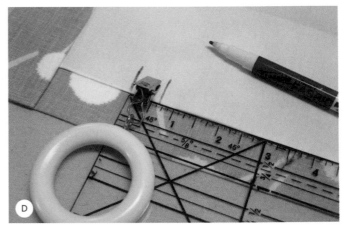

The first mark is inset from the edge, for the return. Use an erasable marker to draw two vertical lines, wide enough for the clips.

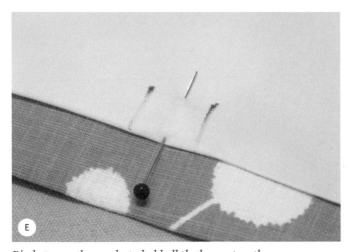

Pin between the marks to hold all the layers together.

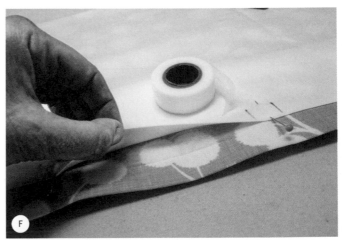

Use iron-on fusing web in the spaces between the marks.

11. Straight stitch on the vertical marks, sewing through all the layers, making two rows of stitching. Use a thread that matches the face fabric. This will create the space where the rings will be clipped.

12. Clip rings to the back of the curtain, between the stitch lines, and install on a pole rod.

TOP *The wave curtain creates pretty columns of fabric when pushed open.*

BOTTOM *When pulled closed, the curtain has a less pronounced wave shape.*

TAB-TOP CURTAIN

Tab-top curtains are a traditional style, but that doesn't make them outdated. It's the perfect look for contemporary décor because of the simplicity and clean lines. You can create a completely unique look just by changing the fabric and hardware. For a shabby chic or country home, use washed linen on rustic wood poles. Change it up for a hip, modern room with bold, graphic patterned fabrics on sleek metal and acrylic rods. For a high-end look, tab tops can meet the challenge with elegant velvet or wool fabrics on glossy painted pole rods.

The basic tab-top curtain can be altered in many ways. Instead of tabs, add ties and install on poles, knobs, hooks, or medallions. Create a tailored curtain with tabs that button down on the front. The size of the tab can be long, short, wide, or skinny. Keep in mind that the wider the tab, the more space it will take up on the rod. Another interesting idea is to space the tabs further apart to create a slouched area. This can look very dramatic in silk fabric!

Tab-top curtains can also be budget friendly. Because it is a flat panel design, fullness is minimal and tabs replace rings, which can really add up when purchasing hardware.

Getting Started

If possible, install the rod above the window and measure the finished width and length. Remember that the curtains will hang below the rod. It is best to raise up the curtains so the window frame or glass does not show.

All curtains look best with a return to the wall on the outside edges to prevent light bleed from the sides. Measure the distance from the wall to the center of the pole for the return.

Tab-top curtains in a vintage-inspired cowboy fabric. Fun for all ages!

The length of the tab depends on the diameter of the pole rod. Use a strip of fabric or ribbon wrapped around the pole to mark the tab size. Plan for six tabs per width of fabric; if the tabs are skinny use more, or use fewer with wider tabs.

To make tab-top curtains operable, use a pole rod with a smooth finish and make the tabs large enough to slide across the pole. The size of the tabs determines the stack-back.

What You Will Need

- decorator fabric
- lining
- drapery weights
- drapery pins
- hardware for installation

Yardage Requirements

If using a print fabric, additional fabric may be needed to match the pattern motif.

FACE FABRIC
Finished length + 12 inches (30.5 cm) for the bottom hem and top facing = cut length

Finished width x 2 fullness ÷ fabric width = number of widths per window (round up)

Cut length x number of widths ÷ 36 inches (91.4 cm) = number of yards (meters) needed

For the tabs, allow ¼ yard (22.9 cm) for every two widths of material used.

LINING
Finished length + 6 inches (15.2 cm) bottom hem = cut length

Cut length x number of widths ÷ 36 inches (91.4 cm) = number of yards (meters) needed

Making a Tab-Top Curtain

1. Follow the instructions for making a basic curtain, adding lining and finishing the hems on the bottom and sides.

2. Measure from the bottom to the top and mark the length. Because the finished length is from the top of the tabs, this is subtracted from the length and then a seam allowance is added.

Finished length - tabs + ½ inch (1.3 cm) = cut length

3. Cut the excess fabric along the marked length. Save the strip of face fabric cut off the top; this will be sewn back on as a facing. Pin the top together. (A)

4. Cut the fabric for the tabs. Use the finished size that you would like the tab to be when it is sewn into the curtain.

Finished width of tab x 2 + 1 inch (2.5 cm) = cut width

Finished length of tab x 2 + 1 inch (2.5 cm) = cut length

5. Sew down the length of each tab using a ½-inch (1.3 cm) seam allowance. Press the seams open and turn right sides out. Press again so that the seam is centered on one side. This creates a front and back. (B)

Cut the hemmed, lined panel to size.

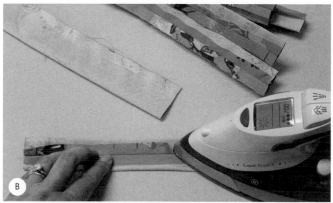

Press the seams open before turning the tabs right sides out.

6. With the curtain face up, pin the tabs to the top edge. One tab at the leading edge is pinned even with the side of the curtain. The tab on the opposite side is inset the amount needed for the curtain to return to the wall. **(C)**

7. Measure from the center of each tab and divide by one less than the number of tabs you are using. For example, on this curtain panel the measurement center-to-center of the two outer tabs is 42 inches (106.7 cm) and there are six tabs. **(D)**

42 divided by 5 = 8.4-inch (21.3 cm) spacing on center for all tabs

8. Pin the remaining tabs to the front. The tabs can also be sewn in place.

9. Use the strip cut from the top after measuring the length to make a facing for the top edge. Cut the strip to 3½ inches (8.9 cm) x the finished panel width + 2 inches (5 cm). Place the facing strip face down over the tabs and pin in place. **(E)** At each corner, tuck under 1 inch (2.5 cm). **(F)**

10. Sew across the top using a ½-inch (1.3 cm) seam allowance. Turn the facing out and press **(G)**, and then turn to the reverse side, folding under the cut edge, and press, making sure the ends are neat and square. **(H)** Finish the facing by hand stitching, machine stitching, or with fabric glue or fusible tape so that it is attached to the lining.

11. To install, slide the tabs across the pole and set in the brackets. Insert a drapery pin hook into the return and attach to the wall. The curtain can be dressed with the spaces coming forward, or pushed back behind the rod. **(I)** (See Chapter 7: Installing Window Treatments.)

C

Inset the outer tab on one side to use as a return to the wall. Be sure to make a pair when working with two panels on a window.

D

Space the tabs evenly across the top.

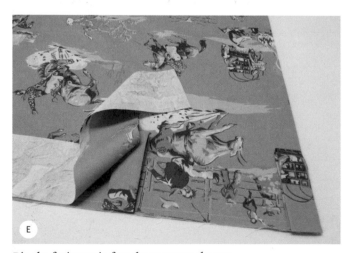

E

Pin the facing strip face down across the top.

F

Fold the facing under on each end before sewing.

G

After sewing, turn the facing up and press.

H

On the reverse side, fold the facing under and press to make a neat hem below the tabs.

The tab-top panel is finished.

I

Insert a drapery pin for the return.

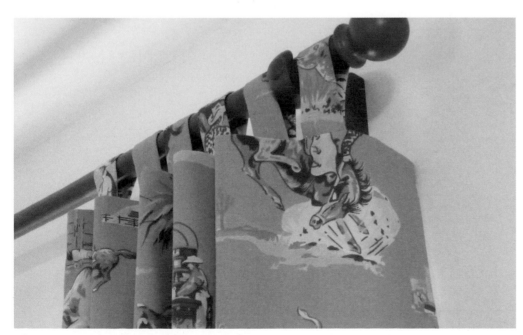

The curtain returns to the wall for a neat finish.

Gathered Curtain Styles

Gathered fabric curtains add texture and softness to the window. This can be achieved by sewing a sleeve or pocket across the top and shirring onto a rod or with shirring or gathering tape that has pull-cords for gathering.

Gathered curtains with tiebacks are a good choice for dormer and inset windows.

ROD POCKET WITH TIEBACKS

Who doesn't love a pretty, gathered curtain with tiebacks? This style is suitable for bedrooms, kitchens, and dormer windows and can even be used for travel trailers! Short lengths work well over radiators or window seats for a feminine, cottage look. Floor-length tieback curtains can be an elegant addition to formal rooms.

Getting Started

Follow the instructions for making a basic curtain. For the top heading, allow enough fabric for a double fold to the back that is large enough to create a pocket for the rod, and extra above the rod for the top ruffle. The amount can vary based on the style of hardware and thickness of the fabric.

Use light- to medium-weight fabric that will gather and drape with ease. Lining is optional. This is the perfect style for sheer and unlined fabrics. If you would like curtains that can be put in the washer and dryer, this is a good choice if the fabrics are washable and colorfast. Prewash all fabrics before sewing.

Determine the size of the rod pocket by wrapping fabric with lining around the rod and pinning together, leaving enough space for the fabric to move easily. The size of the top ruffle should be 1 to 3 inches (2.5 to 7.6 cm).

For this window the curtains meet in the middle and the rod is hidden, so a white adjustable utility rod is a good choice. (A decorative pole rod can also be used. Refer to Chapter 6: Top Treatments for instructions.) Install the rod above the window and measure the finished length, adding for the top ruffle above the rod. If space is limited, this style can be made with just the rod pocket, and no ruffle at the top.

The tiebacks are made in a curved shape to hold the fabric without the tieback being crushed. Fusible fleece is added for extra body and softness.

What You Will Need

- decorator fabric
- lining
- drapery weights
- fusible fleece
- welt cord
- hardware for installation

Yardage Requirements

If using a print fabric, additional fabric may be needed to match the pattern motif.

FACE FABRIC

Finished length + 8 inches (20.3 cm) bottom hem + allowance for rod pocket and top ruffle = cut length

Finished width x 2.5 fullness ÷ fabric width = number of widths per window (round up)

Cut length x number of widths ÷ 36 inches (91.4 cm) = number of yards (meters) needed

LINING

Finished length + 6 inches (15.2 cm) bottom hem + allowance for rod pocket and top ruffle = cut length

Cut length x number of widths ÷ 36 inches (91.4 cm) = number of yards (meters) needed

Making a Rod Pocket with Tiebacks

1. Follow instructions for making a basic curtain, allowing extra fabric for a double-fold heading large enough for the rod pocket and top ruffle.

For example, this curtain has a 1½-inch (3.8 cm) rod pocket and a 2-inch (5 cm) top ruffle, which equals 3½ inches (8.9 cm). To create the double fold, allow 7 inches (17.8 cm).

2. With the panel face down, fold and press the double-fold heading. Measure and mark for the top ruffle. Pin and sew across the bottom edge and along the mark.

Double fold the top heading, measure, and mark the top ruffle. Pin across the mark.

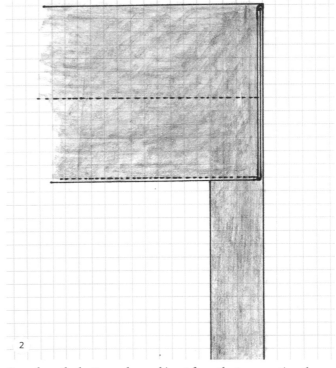

Sew along the bottom edge and inset from the top, creating the rod pocket and top ruffle.

3. Determine the size of the tiebacks by gathering one curtain panel to the finished width and cinching with a soft tape measure, or installing the finished curtain and cutting sample tiebacks from muslin to visualize the finished curtain shape. Generally, tiebacks will be at least 18 inches (45.7 cm) long for single-width panels. Add 4 to 6 inches (10.2 to 15.2 cm) for wider windows with panels using more widths of material. The finished size is based on the look you are trying to achieve.

Note: When using tiebacks, the leading edge will be pulled up. This is a pretty detail but it can show the lining if the curtain is tied back tightly. To make a straight hem, drape a cord on the window, tied back like the curtain will be, and then measure the cord. The length of the cord will be the finished length for the leading edge. The bottom of the curtain panel will angle slightly back to the return edge. In other words, the front edge will be longer, but when the curtains is tied back and dressed, it will all be even at the window.

4. Make a pattern for the tieback using the illustration as a guide. Adjust the size for your project.

5. Place the pattern on the fabric, lining it up so that it is on the straight of grain. Measure and mark for a ½-inch (1.3 cm) seam allowance around the entire pattern. Cut this first piece and then use this to cut the other pieces. (A).

6. When working with pattern motifs, you can feature a design on the tieback. Place the motif near the center right on the right tieback, and the center left on the left tieback.

7. Cut one each for each tieback: face fabric, lining fabric, and fusible fleece. The reverse side can be the same fabric or a plain lining. Cover enough welt cord to go around the edges. (See Chapter 3: Fundamental Techniques.) (B)

8. Iron the face piece to the fusible fleece. Sew the welt cord around the edges. Pin the lining and face piece together, face-to-face, and sew close to the welt cord. Leave an opening for turning right sides out. Turn and press. Close the opening by hand stitching.

9. Sew rings on each end, insetting the ring on the front edge so that it is hidden. (C)

10. To install the curtains, insert the rod inside the rod pocket and push the fabric into gathers. Hang at the window. Straighten the curtain fabric and top ruffle and arrange the gathering evenly. (D)

11. Install small cup hooks into the wall at each side for the tiebacks. Wrap the tiebacks around the curtain panels and hook the rings over the cup hooks. Make sure the tiebacks are hanging at the same angle. Using your hands, smooth and fold the fabric so it falls in even, soft folds behind the tiebacks. (E)

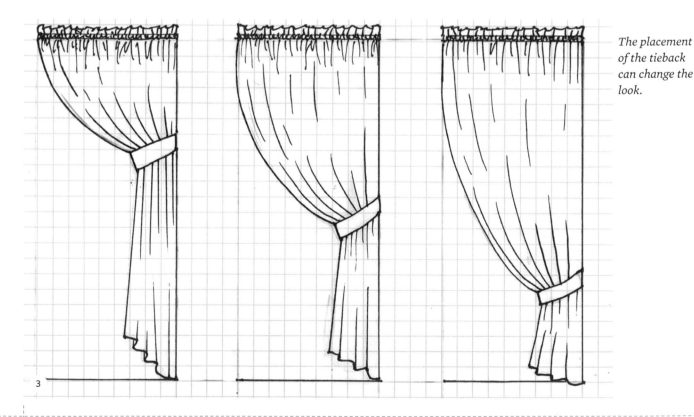

The placement of the tieback can change the look.

3

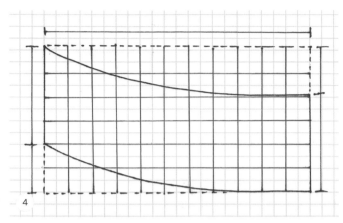

4

Draw the tieback pattern to scale on paper. This is for half the tieback. In this example, each red square is 1 inch (2.5 cm).

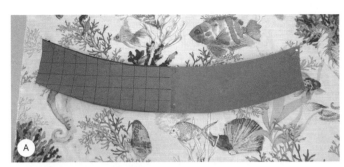

A

Place the pattern on the fabric and cut the shape, adding for a seam allowance.

B

Fronts, backs, fusible fleece, and covered welt cord are ready to sew.

C

Sew rings on each end.

D

Slide the rod into the pocket below the top ruffle. Gather the fabric onto the rod.

E

Dress the fabric so the curtain falls into even folds behind the tieback.

SHIRRING TAPE

This version of a gathered curtain is made with shirring or gathering tape, which is sewn to the back of the curtain panel. Cords within the tape are pulled to create neat gathers.

Getting Started

There are many different types of shirring tape, from a narrow tape with one cord to a wide tape with four cords. There are specialty tapes with smocking and other designs.

The tape is sewn to the back of the heading. Before pulling the cords, tie them securely at each end to prevent them from pulling out of the tape. For large curtains you can tie one end of the cords to a doorknob or table leg for support.

One of the great things about using shirring tape is that it is adjustable. If you leave the cords in place you can untie them to flatten the curtain panel for cleaning or adjusting for a different size. If you choose to leave the cords, sew a small pocket on the back of the curtain to store them.

Shirring tape is used to create the gathered top on these floor-length curtains.

What You Will Need

- decorator fabric
- lining
- shirring tape
- drapery weights
- drapery pins and hardware for installation

Yardage Requirements

If using a print fabric, additional fabric may be needed to match the pattern motif.

FACE FABRIC

Finished length + 8 inches (20.3 cm) bottom hem + allowance for top heading = cut length

Finished width x 2.5 fullness ÷ fabric width = number of widths per window (round up)

Cut length x number of widths ÷ 36 inches (91.4 cm) = number of yards (meters) needed

LINING

Finished length + 6 inches (15.2 cm) bottom hem = cut length

Cut length x number of widths ÷ 36 inches (91.4 cm) = number of yards (meters) needed

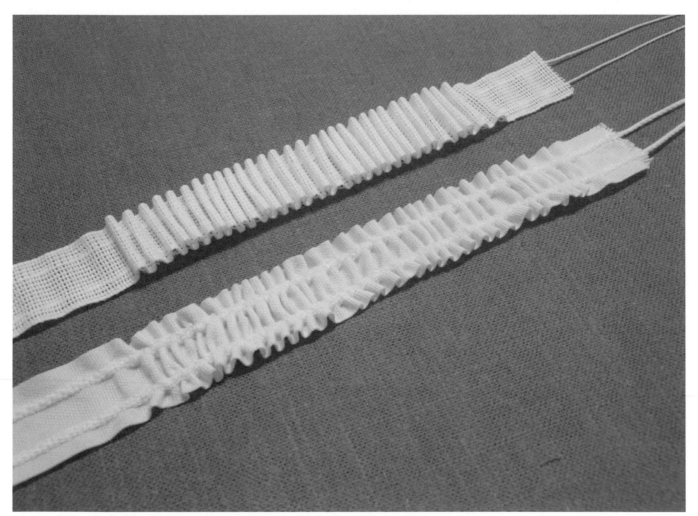

Two common styles of shirring tape used to create pencil pleats or simple gathering.

Making a Shirring Tape Curtain

1. Follow instructions for making a basic curtain. For the top heading, allow enough fabric for a single fold to the back. The amount can vary based on the style of tape and the effect you would like to achieve. Cut away extra fabric.

2. Pin the shirring tape to the back, covering the cut edge of the face fabric. Sew each side and between the cords of the tape, using a matching thread. **(A)**

3. Tie off the cords securely on each end and pull up to the desired size. **(B)**

4. Insert drapery pins into the shirred tape on the back, spacing them 4 to 5 inches (10.2 to 12.7 cm) apart. **(C)**

5. Install and dress the drapery at the window. (See Chapter 7: Installing Window Treatments.)

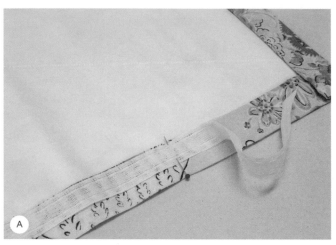

Shirring tape is pinned in place, ready to sew.

Pull the cords to create even gathers and tie off at the finished width.

Stab drapery pin hooks into the tape, making sure they do not stick through to the front. Insert the pin hooks into the ring eyelet.

For a **simple, gathered** top edge, turn the fabric over 1 inch (2.5 cm) and cover the cut edge with the tape. Pin in place and sew the tape on each side and down the center.

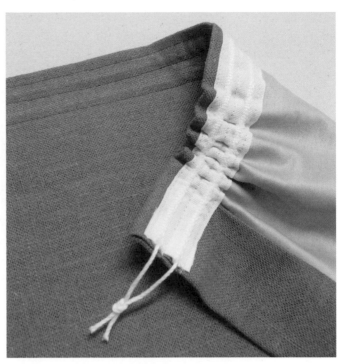

Pull the cords, gathering the fabric across the top.

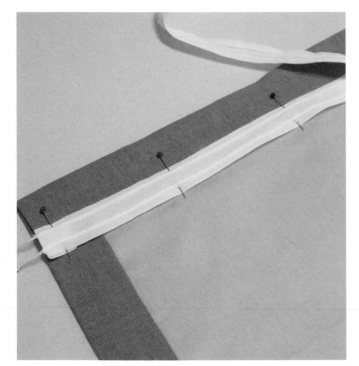

To make a **ruffled** heading, allow for additional fabric above where the tape is sewn. On this panel, 2½ inches (6.4 cm) extra is folded over.

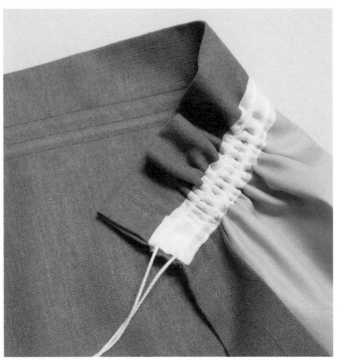

Pull the cords and the ruffle stands above the tape.

RUCHED

This elegant version of a shirred curtain features a ruched, or bunched, heading. It is not functional, so it can be installed on non-traversing hardware like medallions, or even attached to a board with the staples hidden under the ruched heading. Don't be intimidated by this ruched-top showstopper! You will be amazed at how easy it is to make.

Silk fabric is a great choice for this style of curtain.

Getting Started

Use crisp, thin fabrics like silk or chintz for the ruching. Silk fabric was used for this project with interlining added to the main panel for extra body, but it was not needed in the ruched section. Because the ruched heading is a separate piece, you can combine materials such as a velvet or brocade for the main panel and silk at the top for the ruched heading.

What You Will Need

- decorator silk fabric
- lining and interlining
- shirring tape
- drapery weights
- drapery pins and hardware for installation

Yardage Requirements

If using a print fabric, additional fabric may be needed to match the pattern motif.

FACE FABRIC

Finished length + 8 inches (20.3 cm) bottom hem = cut length

Finished width x 2.5 fullness ÷ fabric width = number of widths per window (round up)

Cut length x number of widths ÷ 36 inches (91.4 cm) = number of yards (meters) needed

RUCHED HEADING

36 inches (91.4 cm) of fabric is needed for each curtain width

36 inches (91.4 cm) x number of widths = length needed

LINING

Finished length + 6 inches (15.2 cm) bottom hem = cut length

Cut length x number of widths ÷ 36 inches (91.4 cm) = number of yards (meters) needed

INTERLINING

Finished length - 1 inch (2.5 cm) = cut length

Cut length x number of widths ÷ 36 inches (91.4 cm) = number of yards (meters) needed

Making a Ruched Style

1. Follow instruction for making a basic curtain, adding lining and interlining and finishing the bottom and side hems. Measure from the bottom to the top and mark the finished length. Cut off any excess fabric at the mark. Pin the layers together at the top and serge across to finish the top cut edge. If you do not own a serger, sew across with a straight stitch.

2. Cut fabric for the ruched heading 36 inches (91.4 cm) long by the finished width of the curtain panel plus 1 inch (2.5 cm). For example, if the finished, hemmed curtain is 48 inches (122 cm) wide, cut the piece for the ruched heading 36 inches (91.4 cm) by 49 inches (124.5 cm).

3. Fold in half lengthwise, right sides together and sew down each end using a ½-inch (1.3 cm) seam allowance. (A)

4. Turn right sides out to create an 18-inch (45.7 cm) finished piece. You do not need to press the seams. Pin together along the cut edges and serge or sew together.

5. Place the finished curtain panel face down and place the ruched heading piece even with the top and with the serged edges together. (B)

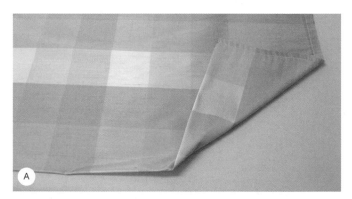

Fold the piece for the ruched heading in half lengthwise, face-to-face, and sew each end.

Place on the back of the finished panel, lining up the edges.

6. Mark a line 4 inches (10.2 cm) from the top. Pin along the line and sew across. (C)

7. From the back of the curtain panel, turn the ruched piece toward the top and press flat. (D)

8. Turn the panel face up and pin shirring tape along the serged seam. Be sure to tie off the cords on one end. The ruched top piece will be flat, above the shirring tape. (E)

9. Sew the shirring tape to the panel. Sew along each side and down the center of the tape. After it is sewn, pull the cords to gather the curtain. Measure to size if making a pair, so that they both are the same width. (F)

10. Flip the top piece over to the front. (G)

Note: At this point you could add pin hooks and hang the curtain at the window for a pretty gathered curtain with an attached valance.

11. Use your hands to fluff and bunch the top heading for the ruched look. Don't try to make it too symmetrical; it should be unstructured and soft. (H)

12. Use a tacking or tag gun to secure the heading to the panel or stab stich throughout the ruching to hold it in place. Make sure the horizontal stitch line is covered.

13. Insert pin hooks into the heading on the reverse side, spaced 4 to 6 inches (10.2 to 15.2 cm) apart. (I)

Mark and sew 4 inches (10.2 cm) from the top edge, sewing the ruched piece to the back of the curtain panel.

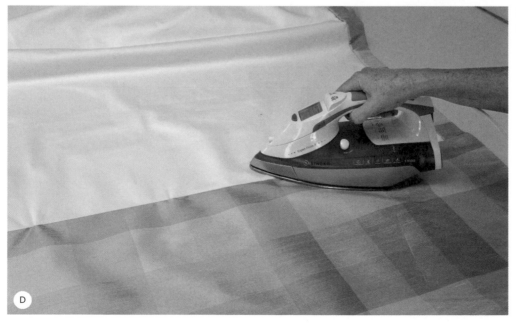

Turn up the top piece and press along the seam on the back.

Pin shirring tape along the top serged edges.

Pull the cords to gather the curtain.

Flip over the top section.

Fluff and bunch the fabric to create the ruched look.

Insert pin hooks into the shirring tape area on the back of the curtain.

The finished ruched heading should look unstructured and spontaneous.

Pleated Curtain Styles

Pleated curtains or draperies are a timeless, classic window fashion that will never go out of style. There are many styles of pleats, which are sewn across the top of the fabric panel with even spacing. Pleated curtains can be traditional and formal in appearance, or cute and casual, depending on the fabrics used. They can be unlined, lined, or interlined. There are so many options!

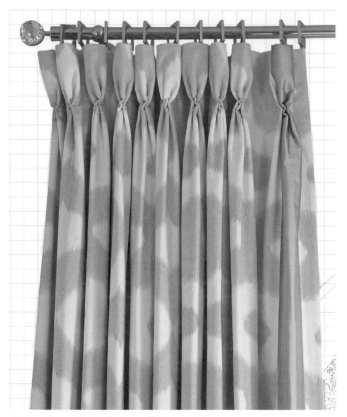

Goblet pleats dress the top of this curtain.

Buckram is used to create a crisp pleat.

A stiffener such as buckram or crinoline can be folded into the heading to help the pleats keep their shape. This is especially important for operable curtains, but you can also make pleated curtains without buckram.

There are two ways to add buckram to the top heading of the curtain: a double fold of fabric with the buckram included, or a single fold of fabric, which is known as the "low-bulk" method. Both options are shown and work equally well for pleated curtains. Use the double-fold heading if buckram is omitted.

To make curtains from sheer fabric without lining, reverse the steps by making the double fold of fabric with the buckram first, then measuring the length plus a hem allowance, cutting off excess fabric, finishing the bottom hem, and then finishing the side hems last.

Pleated curtains can be made to fit the window so that they can be drawn open and closed, and installed on traversing hardware or decorative poles with rings. They can also be purely decorative, pleated and hung on each side of the window in a fixed position. The beauty of fabric panels alone on each side of the window can be a great design choice, and curtains are a lovely complement over blinds or shutters, or under top treatments.

To create pleats, fullness is figured into the fabric calculations. The most common fullness ratio for pleated curtains is two and a half times, but this can vary based on the style of pleats and by using more or less fullness.

When planning pleated curtains it looks best to raise the hardware above the window and extend it at least a few inches on each side if room allows. You must also consider "stack-back," which is the space taken up by the drapery when it is drawn open. If there isn't enough room to extend the hardware past the window and onto the wall, you will have more of the curtain covering the window glass when it is opened.

UNDERSTANDING PLEATS AND SPACES

Before you calculate the pleats and spaces, you must know what type of hardware will be used, and whether the curtains will be one-way or two-way draw (also known as a split draw). A one-way draw is typical for a sliding door, with a large curtain panel opening to one side. A two-way draw has a pair of curtain panels, one on each side, and closes to the center.

Some curtain rods, known as "traverse rods," operate with a cord or baton, and the curtain hangs from small carriers that slide back and forth. You can also use simple decorative pole rods in wood or metal with rings that slide onto the pole. The rings will have small eyelets for attaching the curtain with pin hooks or clips.

To calculate pleats and spaces, you must know whether your hardware has an "overlap." The overlap is made up of two sturdy "master carriers" at the center that allow the curtain panels to close neatly without a light gap. Most traverse rods will have an overlap master carrier. The overlap size is normally 3½ inches (8.9 cm) and is included in the calculations for this style.

Here is a simple way to understand how pleats and spaces are figured. When you look at a pleated curtain, the flat areas or spaces between the pleats will cover the rod. The excess fabric or fullness beyond what is needed to cover the rod is then evenly divided into pleats.

Getting Started

When making multiple-width panels, it is important to place the seams to the back of a pleat or to the side of a space, so it is less obvious, and never within a pleat. It is acceptable to adjust the size of your pleats slightly so that you can manage seams, while keeping the spaces even. For example, if you have a three-width panel with two seams, you may have 5-inch (12.7 cm) pleats on the first width, 4¾-inch (12.1 cm) pleats on the next width, and 5-inch (12.7 cm) pleats on the third width while keeping the spaces all the same. You may want to make a pleating template before you cut and sew fabrics so that you can plan the seam placement.

What You Will Need

- decorator fabric
- lining
- buckram
- drapery weights
- pin hooks
- hardware for installation

This rod has overlapping master carriers. The curtains will overlap in the center.

Yardage Requirements

FACE FABRIC

Finished length + 16 inches (40.6 cm) if using the double-fold heading or + 12 inches (30.5 cm) for the low-bulk heading = cut length

Finished width x 2.5 fullness ÷ fabric width = number of widths per window (round up)

Cut length x number of widths ÷ 36 inches (91.4 cm) = number of yards (meters) needed

If using a print fabric, additional fabric may be needed to match the pattern motif.

FACE FABRIC WITH PATTERN REPEATS

Finished length + 16 inches (40.6 cm) if using the double-fold heading or + 12 inches (30.5 cm) for the low-bulk heading ÷ the pattern repeat = number of pattern repeats for each cut

Pattern repeat x number of repeats = cut length

Finished width x 2.5 fullness ÷ fabric width = number of widths per window (round up)

Cut length x number of widths ÷ 36 inches (91.4 cm) = number of yards (meters) needed

LINING

Finished length + 6 inches (15.2 cm) if using the double-fold heading or + 9 inches (22.9 cm) if using the low-bulk heading = cut length

Cut length x number of widths ÷ 36 inches (91.4 cm) = number of yards needed

Making a Double-Fold Heading

1. Follow instructions for making a basic curtain, adding lining and drapery weights at the side hems and seams. Measure from the bottom edge to the top, folding over the extra fabric and pressing a crease at the finished length. Cut off any excess fabric, leaving 8 inches (20.3 cm) folded over. (A)

2. Turn the curtain panel so that the heading is facing you, lining side up. Cut a piece of buckram 7 inches (17.8 cm) more than the finished panel width. Press a double fold in the top heading and place the buckram inside the fold, folding over the 3½ inches (8.9 cm) of extra buckram on each end (this provides more body for the overlap and return). (B) You can finish the heading with the side hems under or on top of the double fold. Either way is correct. (C)

3. Secure the heading with pins. You can use iron-on fusing web or fabric glue under the heading, but it isn't required because sewing the pleats will hold the layers together.

4. Sew around the corners, and finish the side hems. The curtain is ready to be pleated.

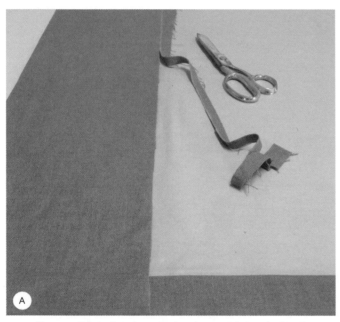

Cut off excess fabric, leaving 8 inches (20.3 cm) for the heading.

Fold the buckram over on each end for added body at the overlap and return areas.

Buckram is included inside the double-fold heading.

Making a Low-Bulk Heading

1. Follow instructions for making a basic curtain, adding lining and drapery weights at the side hems and seams. Measure from the bottom edge to the top, adding 4 inches (10.2 cm) to the finished length. Mark and cut off any excess fabric.

2. Turn the curtain panel so that the heading is facing you, lining side up. Cut a piece of iron-on buckram 7 inches (17.8 cm) wider than the finished panel width. Iron the buckram to the back of the fabric, even with the top edge and folding over 3½ inches (8.9 cm) of extra buckram at each end. (A)

3. Fold over and press the fabric with the buckram attached, so that the top edge of the buckram is even with the finished length.

4. Measure and cut off the lining 3½ inches (8.9 cm) longer than the finished length. (B)

5. Fold under the lining so that there is a ½-inch (1.3 cm) reveal of the face fabric at the top. Press the lining so that it is neat and flat. The bottom cut edge of the lining should be even with the bottom of the buckram. (C)

6. Secure the lining to the back of the heading with iron-on fusing web. (D)

7. Fold and press the side hems over the buckram heading. (E)

8. Sew around the corners, and finish the side hems. The curtain is ready to be pleated.

Mark and cut off the lining 3½ inches (8.9 cm) past the top of the curtain.

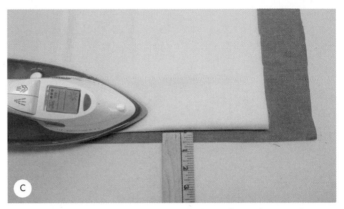

Fold under the lining ½ inch (1.3 cm) down from the top edge.

Attach the lining to the back with iron-on fusing web.

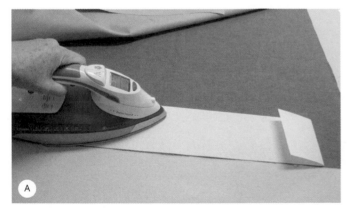

Use fusible buckram for a low-bulk heading.

Fold and press the side hems and across the top.

Calculating Pleats and Spaces
To begin, answer these questions:

1. *What type of hardware am I using?*

   - Traverse rod
   - Decorative pole with rings (wood or metal)

2. *How will it traverse?*

   - Two-way draw from the center
   - One-way to the left or right only

Before you begin calculating pleats and spaces you will need to know the finished rod measurement, the size of the overlap master carrier (if using a traverse rod), and the projection of the hardware or "return." Make copies of the calculations on the following pages to use as worksheets, filling out the information for your specific project.

The following list shows the average number of pleats per width of material, based on a curtain using two and a half times fullness. Use this as a guideline as you work on your calculations.

1 width = 5 pleats

$1\frac{1}{2}$ widths = 7 pleats

2 widths = 10 pleats

$2\frac{1}{2}$ widths = 12 or 13 pleats

3 widths = 15 pleats

$3\frac{1}{2}$ widths = 17 or 18 pleats

Spaces between the pleats should be $3\frac{1}{2}$ to 4 inches (8.9 to 10.2 cm) and each pleat will use $4\frac{1}{2}$ to 6 inches (11.5 to 15.2 cm) of fabric.

Making a Traverse Curtain with Two-Way Draw
Two curtain panels will be pleated to fit the right and left sides of the rod plus overlap in the center and return to the wall.

Width of rod from outer edges = _____ + _____ overlap size + _____ return (there are two returns on this rod so double the measurement) = _____ ÷ 2 = _____ finished size of each curtain panel. After the pleats are sewn in, each panel will need to measure to this finished size.

PLEATS
Measure across one flat, unpleated panel = _____ - _____ finished size = _____ amount used for pleats. Divide by the number of pleats (based on the average of 5 pleats per width of material) = _____ size of each pleat

SPACES
Measure across the flat, unpleated panel = _____ - $3\frac{1}{2}$-inch (8.9 cm) overlap - _____ returns - _____ amount used for pleats. Divided by the number of spaces (one less than the number of pleats) = _____ size of each space

Making a Traverse Curtain with One-Way Draw
One curtain panel will be pleated to fit across the front of the rod plus a return to the wall on one side.

Width of rod from outer edges = _____ + _____ return = _____ finished size. After the pleats are sewn in, each panel will need to measure to this finished size.

PLEATS
Measure across the flat, unpleated panel = _____ - _____ finished size = _____ amount used for pleats. Divide by the number of pleats (based on the average of 5 pleats per width of material) = _____ size of each pleat

SPACES
Measure across the flat, unpleated panel = _____ - _____ return - _____ amount used for pleats. Divide by the number of spaces (one less than the number of pleats) = _____ of each space

Making a Curtain for a Decorative Pole Rod with Rings and Two-Way Draw
Two drapery panels will be pleated to fit the right and left sides of the rod and meet in the center. There isn't an overlap carrier. Extra width is added for ease, or "spring back," on this style of rod.

Width of rod the curtain will cover (do not include finials) = _____ + 2 inches (5 cm) for ease + _____ return (there are two returns on this rod so double the measurement) ÷ 2 = _____ finished size of each curtain panel. After the pleats are sewn in, each panel will need to measure to this finished size.

PLEATS

Measure across the flat, unpleated panel = _____ - finished size = _____ amount used for pleats. Divide by the number of pleats (based on the average of 5 pleats per width of fabric) = _____ size of each pleat

SPACES

Measure across the flat, unpleated panel = _____ - 2 inches (5 cm) for ease - _____ returns - _____ amount used for pleats. Divide by the number of spaces (one less than the number of pleats) = _____ size of each space

Making a Curtain for a Decorative Pole Rod with Rings and One-Way Draw

One drapery panel will be pleated to fit across the front of the rod plus returns to the wall on one side.

Width of rod the curtain will cover (do not include finials) = _____ + 2 inches (5 cm) for ease + _____ return = _____ finished size. After the pleats are sewn in, the curtain panel will need to measure to this finished size.

PLEATS

Measure across the flat, unpleated panel = _____ - size that it needs to be finished after pleating = _____ divided by the number of pleats (based on the average of 5 pleats per width of fabric) = _____ size of each pleat

SPACES

Measure across the flat, unpleated panel = _____ - 2 inches (5 cm) for ease - _____ return - _____ amount used for pleats. Divide by the number of spaces (one less than the number of pleats) = _____ size of each space

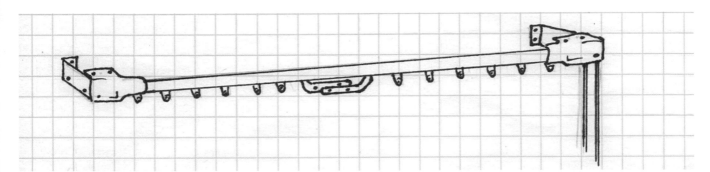

Two-way draw traverse rod.

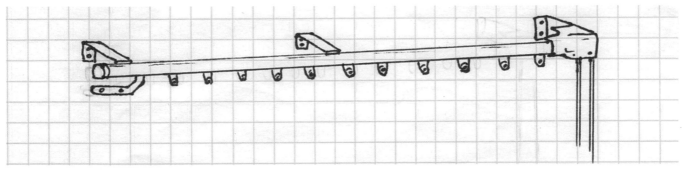

One-way draw traverse rod.

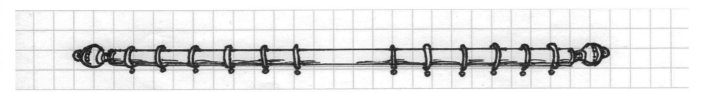

An example of a decorative pole rod with rings.

SEWING PLEATS

1. Use pins to mark the pleats and spaces. (A)

2. Sew a vertical seam from the top to the bottom of the heading. To keep the pleats even at the top, place the pleat under the presser foot and turn the hand wheel so that the needle is inserted into the pleat ½ inch (1.3 cm) down from the top, backstitch, and then sew. This will keep the layers from shifting. Sew 4 inches (10.2 cm) from the top to the bottom. When you are at the base of the pleat, backstitch again. (B)

3. After the pleats are sewn, measure to check the finished width. If it is not accurate you can adjust the width by taking out a few pleats and sewing again. Don't stress over fractions; it will not be noticeable when the curtain is hanging! (C)

Pin together the pleats across the heading.

Seat the needle down into the fabric ½ inch (1.3 cm) from the top, then backstitch and continue sewing to the bottom of the heading.

Check the measurement after the pleats are sewn.

Different Styles of Pleats

A variety of pleat styles can be created by tacking with a needle and thread at the top, bottom, or center of the pleat. Use a long needle and two strands of heavy thread. Knot the thread and start by stabbing the needle inside one of the folds and out the side; this will hide the knot on the inside. Continue stitching to form one of the pleats shown on page 89. When the pleat stitching is finished, stitch a knot and stab the needle into a thick area and out, pulling the knot into the fabric and trimming the thread.

Stab the needle through the thickness of the pleat and then trim away the excess thread.

French

The French pleat, also known as a pinch pleat, is divided into three sections, or "fingers." Pinch the pleat together and stitch at the base of the pleat. If using buckram, you will find it easier to stitch below the buckram. You can also stitch together at the top. This is optional. A two-finger French pleat can also be made using the same technique.

Goblet

The pleat is tacked at the bottom like a French pleat, and then opened up and rounded at the top. To keep the rounded shape, foam or batting can be stuffed into the pleat.

Euro

The pleat is divided into two or three sections and tacked at the top only by stab stitching from one side to the other, or by whipstitching the top edge to hold the folds together.

Cartridge

The pleat has a simple, rounded shape and is not pinched or folded into sections. Stuff the pleats with rolled-up buckram or foam. Pipe insulation found in the plumbing department of the hardware store makes a great stuffing for cartridge pleats.

Butterfly

The pleat is divided into two equal sections and tacked 2 inches (5 cm) down from the top, in the center of the heading.

French pleat.

Goblet pleat.

Euro pleat.

Cartridge pleat.

Butterfly pleat.

Inverted Pleats

Not all pleats are formed on the front of the curtain. With inverted pleats, the fullness is to the back. This style is tailored and can be functional, or used as a decorative side panel. Use medium-weight home decorator fabrics that are not too heavy or stiff. Buckram is used, but it can be omitted for a softer look.

1. Follow the instructions for making a pleated curtain with a double-fold heading up to the point of sewing the pleats. The only changes will be in how the pleats are sewn.

2. Figure the pleats and spaces. The only difference when using inverted pleats is that you can have larger spaces than other pleat styles. If you want the curtains to traverse, plan for 5 inches (12.7 cm) or less in each pleat and 5- to 6-inch (12.7 to 15.2 cm) spaces. For stationary panels, you can have larger pleats.

3. Begin by marking the return, pleats, and spaces. The first space at the leading edge should match all the other spaces.

4. Pin and sew the pleats with the fullness to the reverse side. (A) (B)

5. Flatten out a pleat evenly on the back. From the front, carefully machine stitch "in-the-ditch" down the center of the pleat (C), backtacking at the beginning and end of the seam. Sew from the top to the bottom of the heading with a thread that matches the face fabric. (D)

6. After all the pleats are sewn, insert pin hooks into the seam on the back of each pleat. (E)

7. The inverted pleat curtains are ready to install. (F)

With inverted pleats, the flat spaces between the pleats roll to the front.

Pin the pleats for sewing with the fullness to the reverse side.

The curtain is flat on the front, with the pleats facing the back.

Flatten the pleat on the back and stitch down the center of the seam from the front.

The pleats are sewn. From the back you can see the stitch line in the center.

Insert pin hooks into the stitch line on the back of each pleat.

Install the pin hook into the eyelet on the ring.

This bathroom has a window curtain and shower curtain with inverted pleats.

Café curtains add privacy over the sink in this kitchen,
but can be opened for the full view

SCALLOPED SPACES

Curtains do not need to be floor length or even go to the top of the entire window. When only the bottom of the window needs to be covered for privacy, café curtains are the answer! It is most common for café curtains to cover the bottom half of the window, but the length can be customized to cover more or less of the window, depending on how much privacy is needed. Any type of heading can be used for café curtains: gathered, pleated, or flat styles.

Keep in mind that the top heading of the café curtain will be at eye level. For this reason it's fun to add a little extra "wow" factor to the heading, like the scalloped spaces on this curtain at left. A retro fabric was used to complement the 1970s kitchen tile.

Café curtains can be mounted inside or outside the frame. If you are uncertain of the length, tape paper or muslin over the bottom of the window to see how it will look from both the inside and the outside of your home.

Getting Started

Before you start, figure the pleats and spaces using the calculations found in the previous section (see "Making a Curtain for a Decorative Pole Rod with Rings and Two-Way Draw"). This will be used to create the template for the top heading. If using a patterned fabric, you may be able to plan the pleats and spaces to match the pattern. This isn't always possible but it's certainly worth a try!

What You Will Need

- decorator fabric
- lining
- buckram (iron-on)
- drapery weights
- pin hooks
- hardware for installation

Yardage Requirements

If using a print fabric, additional fabric may be needed to match the pattern motif.

FACE FABRIC
Finished length + 14 inches (35.6 cm) = cut length

Finished width x 2.5 fullness ÷ fabric width = number of widths per window (round up)

Cut length x number of widths ÷ 36 inches (91.4 cm) = number of yards (meters) needed

LINING
Finished length + 6 inches (15.2 cm) = cut length

Cut length x number of widths ÷ 36 inches (91.4 cm) = number of yards (meters) needed

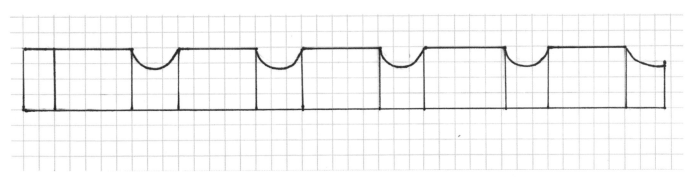

On the template, draw a scalloped shape in each space. This is an example of how the template will look.

Making Scalloped Spaces

1. Mark the pleat and spaces on a piece of iron-on buckram. Draw a scallop shape in each marked space. The leading edge will only use half of the scalloped shape. The return does not need to be scalloped. Cut out the scallops. (A)

2. Seam fabrics together if using multiple widths. Measure and mark from the bottom of the fabric to the top, adding 8½ inches (21.6 cm) to the finished length (4-inch [10.2 cm] doubled hem and ½-inch [1.3 cm] seam allowance). Cut off excess fabric and set aside. This will be used for the facing along the back of the pleats.

3. Using the excess fabric cut off in the last step, cut to 5 inches (12.7 cm). The width stays the same. Sew to the top front of thc lining fabric. The facing can be topstitched or sewn face down and flipped over even with the top. (B)

4. Iron the buckram with scallops to the back of the curtain fabric, inset ½ inch (1.3 cm) from the top and allowing 3 inches (7.6 cm) past each end for the side hems.

5. Place the lining with the facing attached face up and top with the curtain fabric face down, with the buckram over the facing and the edges even. (C)

6. Pin across the top and machine stitch along the top edge, following the shape and sewing next to the buckram. (D)

7. Cut away fabric ¼ inch (6 mm) from the edge of the buckram. (E)

8. Turn the curtain right sides out and press the top so that the edges are neat and flat. Press on the front and back. (F)

A

Cut away the scalloped shapes from the spaces marked on the buckram.

B

A strip of the main fabric is sewn to the top of the lining.

C

Place the lining fabric with the facing attached and the main fabric with the buckram attached face-to-face, lining up the top edges.

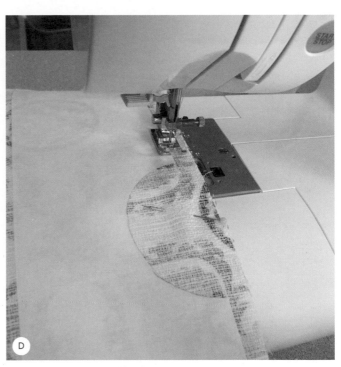

D

Sew next to the shaped buckram.

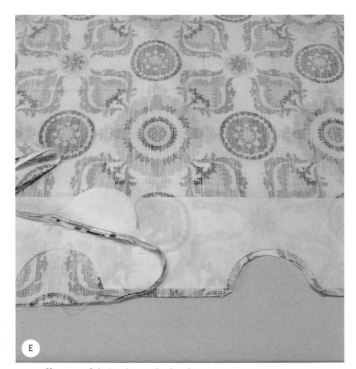

E

Cut off excess fabric above the buckram.

F

Press the scalloped heading.

9. With the curtain face down, measure the finished length from the top straight edge (not from the scallop) to the bottom. Fold over excess fabric and press. Fold again for a 4-inch (10.2 cm) doubled hem and pin. Repeat for the lining fabric, allowing for a 3-inch (7.6 cm) doubled hem. Finish the hems. (G)

10. Turn over side hems and add weights at each bottom corner. Pin and finish the side hems. The curtain is ready to be pleated. (H)

11. Pin together the flat areas between the scallops to form the pleats. Sew from the top to the bottom of the buckram. Hand stitch at the base of each pleat under the buckram (I) and at the top (J) to create French pleats. You can also use any other pleat style. (See "Different Styles of Pleats.")

12. Insert drapery pins into the back of the pleats and install on the hardware.

Measure and mark for the bottom hems in the main fabric and lining.

Add a 1½-inch (3.8 cm) doubled hem on each side.

Pinch together the pleat and hand stitch at the bottom.

Stitch together the top to form a neat, triple pleat.

Continue tacking all the pleats.

This curtain is pleated to the pattern.

Small-diameter pole rods and rings are a good choice for café curtains. Add drapery pins to the back of each pleat and insert the pin into the eyelet on the ring.

BOX PLEATS WITH GROMMETS

Grommet panels are very popular but sometimes they are just too plain and flat. This curtain style combines grommets with box pleats, and can be used for functional curtains or purely decorative side panels. With generous fullness and topstitched pleats, this style is eye-catching and new, something different from the everyday curtain.

Getting Started

Box pleats require more fullness than typical curtains. Allow two and a half to three times the finished width. For the top heading, allow enough fabric for a double fold to the back. Buckram is not needed in this curtain.

Use light- to medium-weight decorator fabrics. Box-pleated grommet curtains can be lined or unlined. Print fabrics can be very eye-catching if pleated to the pattern, while solid fabrics can show off the dimension and shadows created by the pleats.

Select a rod that is a smaller diameter than the grommets, so the curtain will slide easily. Plan to use grommets with an inside diameter of 30 to 40 percent more than the rod diameter if the curtain will be operable.

Like with any grommet curtain, always plan for an even number of grommets so that the outside and inside edges both face in the same direction toward the wall.

Measure the distance from the wall to the center of the pole for the return and leading edge. You want to make sure the leading edge clears the window frame or other window treatments under the curtain.

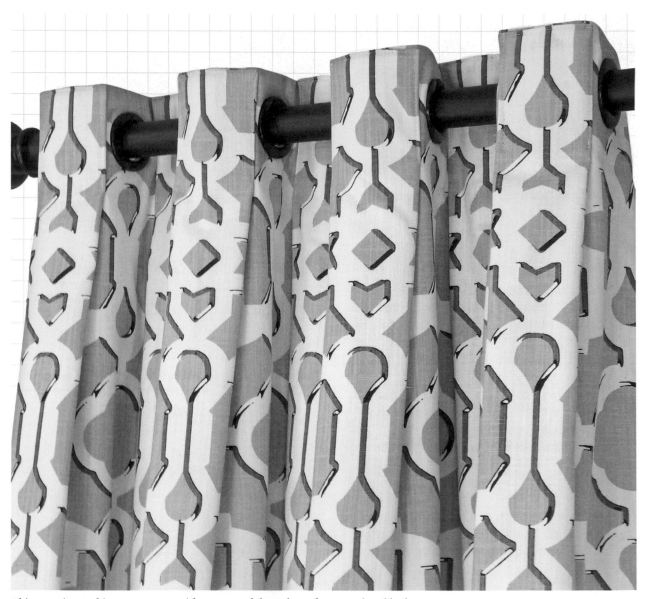

This curtain combines grommets with structured, box pleats for an updated look.

What You Will Need

- decorator fabric
- lining
- grommets
- drapery weights
- tools and hardware for installation

Yardage Requirements

Make a template of the pleats and spaces first to determine the exact amount you will need for the finished width.

If using a print fabric, additional fabric may be needed to match the pattern motif.

FACE FABRIC

Finished length + 16 inches (40.6 cm) for the bottom hem and top heading = cut length

Finished width x at least 2.5 fullness ÷ fabric width = number of widths per window (round up)

Cut length x number of widths ÷ 36 inches (91.4 cm) = number of yards (meters) needed

LINING

Finished length + 6 inches (15.2 cm) bottom hem = cut length

Cut length x number of widths ÷ 36 inches (91.4 cm) = number of yards (meters) needed

Making Box Pleats with Grommets

1. Begin by making a template for the top heading on a strip of paper or piece of buckram, following the illustration below. Mark pleats and spaces where the grommets will be placed. If using a print fabric, look at the horizontal repeat to see if it can be pleated to pattern.

A polyester fabric with a linen look was used for this unlined curtain. Solid fabrics are a great choice for this style.

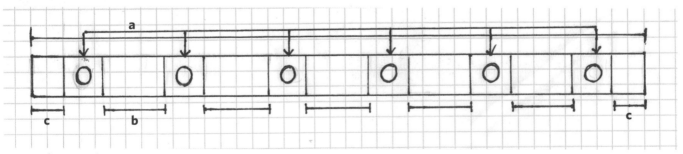

Make a template.
a. Space between grommets
b. Pleats
c. Side hems

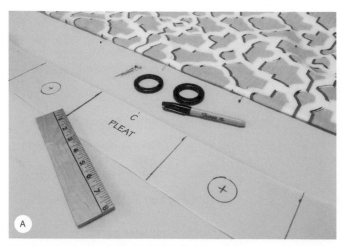

Check the template with the fabric before cutting.

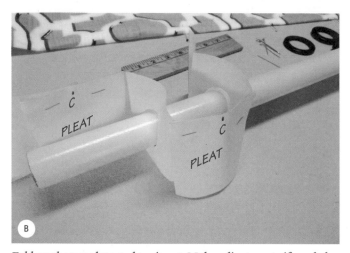

Fold up the template and try it out. Make adjustments if needed.

2. Mark where the seams will fall on the template (based on the fabric width) and then use this to lay out your fabrics. You may need to trim away fabric off the leading edge or slightly adjust the spaces and pleats, especially if trying to pleat to the pattern. (A)

3. Check the template with the fabric. Mark side hems and cut away any excess fabric.

4. Cut out holes in the template where the grommets will be and fold up the pattern. Staple the pleats and check the size by threading the template onto a pole or yardstick. (B)

5. Follow instructions for making a pleated curtain with a double-fold heading. For this curtain, a doubled 4-inch (10.2 cm) heading was used. You can adjust this based on the grommet size. For example, a 3-inch (7.6 cm) doubled heading could be used with smaller grommets.

6. Turn the curtain panel so that the heading is facing you, lining side up. Use the template to mark the grommet holes. Remove the template and staple inside of each hole. This will hold the fabric together when cutting the holes. (C)

7. Set the grommets following the instructions in this section for making a grommet panel. When all the grommets are set, the curtain is ready to be pleated.

8. Use the template to mark the pleats. Fold the pleats and pin. (D)

9. Sew the pleats from the top to the bottom of the heading, backstitching at the beginning and end of each seam.

10. Flatten out each pleat on the front. Topstitch neatly around the edges using a matching thread. (E)

11. The curtain is finished and ready to install. (F)

12. Thread the rod through the grommets with the outside and inside edges turned toward the back. (G)

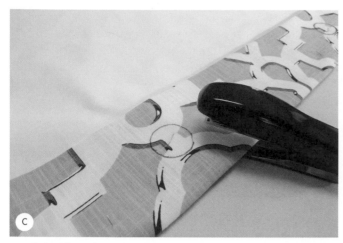

Staple inside each circle mark.

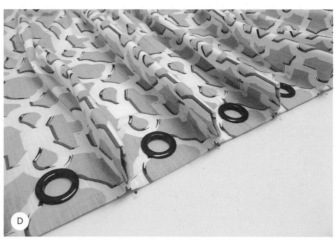

Fold and pin pleats between grommets, using the template as a guide.

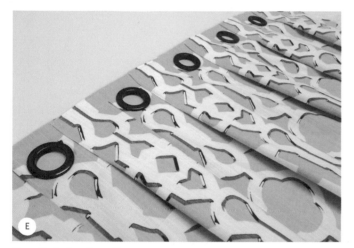

Topstitch the pleats flat.

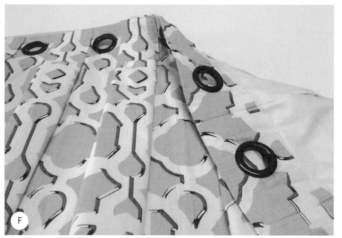

After the pleats are topstitched, the curtain is ready to install.

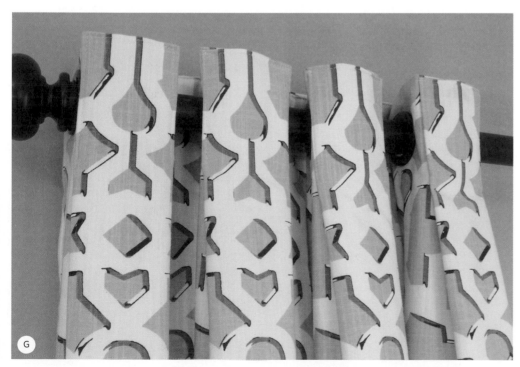

Box pleats stack back neatly on the rod.

Arched Panels on Medallions

Arched windows are the focal point of a room but are often left unadorned because designing and making arched window treatments can be overwhelming. By following the instructions you will be able to master arched curtains and the method shown can be translated for arched, pleated top treatments and shades.

There are several common styles of arched windows, including the true half circle, quarter circle, elliptical, and eyebrow shapes as well as triangular, octagonal, and other unique shapes. All can be dressed with draperies.

Getting Started

Arched draperies are not functional, and are for decorative purposes only. For a traversing drapery, consider installing on a horizontal rod above the arch or combine arched panels with a blind or shade for privacy and light control. This style requires room above the arch for the medallions to be mounted to the wall and the spaces between the pleats to slouch into swag shapes without showing the frame. If you do not have room above the window you can still use this style with flat spaces shaped to fit the arch.

There are two key steps in making an arched drapery: (1) thorough, accurate measurements and (2) a detailed paper pattern. Once you draft the pattern the concept will be clear; it will all make sense! Sewing will be easier than you may think. Arched curtains are made "top down," where the hem is added last, so you will not follow the basic curtain-making techniques shown earlier in this section.

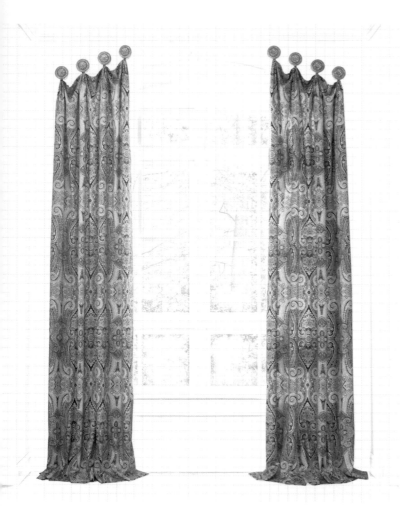

Arched curtains are mounted on decorative medallions. Spaces between the pleats slouch, for more texture and interest.

Curtains can be installed above the arch on a straight rod.

What You Will Need

- pattern paper
- decorator fabric
- lining
- drapery weights
- hardware for installation

Yardage Requirements

A more accurate way to figure the yardage is to make the pattern first, and then you will know exactly how many widths you will need for each panel.

If using a print fabric, additional fabric may be needed to match the pattern motif.

FACE FABRIC

Finished length at the longest point + 16 inches (40.6 cm) = cut length

Finished width (curtain only, not the window) x 2.5 fullness ÷ fabric width = number of widths for one curtain panel (round up)

Cut length x number of widths ÷ 36 inches (91.4 cm) = number of yards (meters) needed for one curtain panel (multiply x 2 for the pair)

LINING

Finished length at the longest + 6 inches (15.2 cm) bottom hem = cut length

Cut length x number of widths ÷ 36 inches (91.4 cm) = number of yards (meters) needed

Making the Paper Pattern

1. Measure the window, making notes of the width from side-to-side (a), the length from the tallest point at the center of the arch to the floor (c), and the length from the lowest point on the side of the window to the floor (b). Measure from a horizontal point, such as a window sash or frame, to the floor (d); this will be used for marking the length and keeping the pattern level.

2. Measure above the frame to the ceiling and on each side. Plan to extend the curtains on the left and right sides past the frame slightly and measure how wide the curtains will be when finished. A cord can be draped over the window to help visualize how the curtains will look.

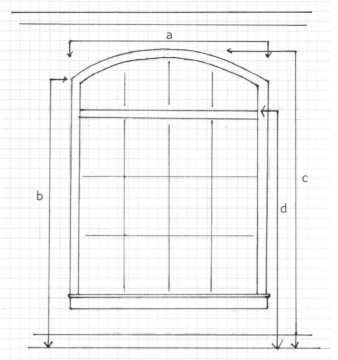

a. Width from side-to-side **b.** Top corner to the floor (measure both sides) **c.** Center of the arch to the floor **d.** Horizontal point for reference

1

Measure the arched window.

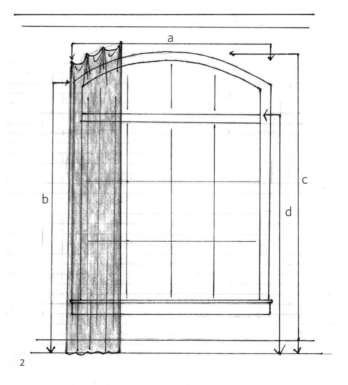

2

This sketch shows the proportions of the finished curtain. For this project, the drapery was 18 inches (45.7 cm) wide. Drape cords on the window to figure the finished size. Be sure to measure the finished length for the leading edge at this point to the floor.

3. Draw a paper template of half of the arched window by taping paper or heavy plastic over the window frame and sketching the shape with a permanent marker. You can also draft the arched shape based on the measurements if it is a true arch.

4. Hang the arched template on the wall and mark where each medallion will be placed above the frame. Drape a cord from each mark, representing the finished curtain width and the draped, slouched areas between each pleat. (A)

5. Stretch out the draped cord and measure. This is the size that the spaces will be. (B)

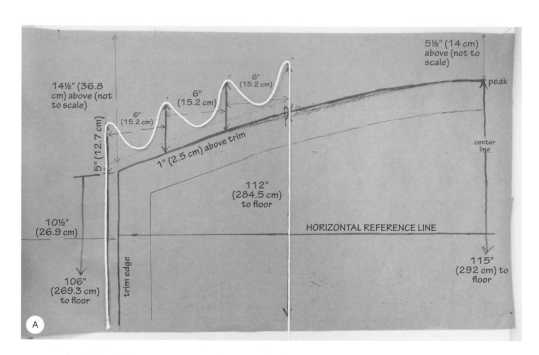

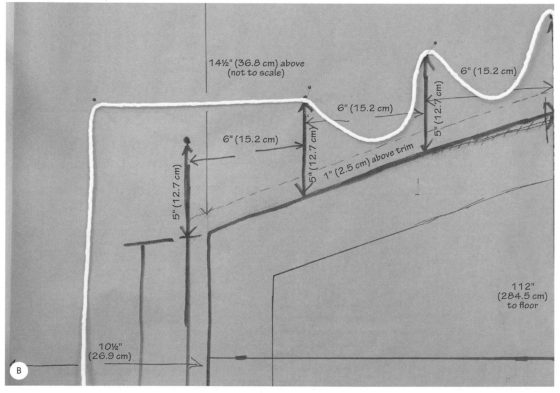

Singer Sewing Custom Curtains, Shades, and Top Treatments

6. Remove the template and connect the spaces between the marked medallions across the top. Cut out the pattern along the sides and top. Make one additional pattern to use as a guide for installing the medallions at the window. (C)

7. Draw vertical lines from each mark for the medallions down to the bottom. Each line represents a pleat. (D)

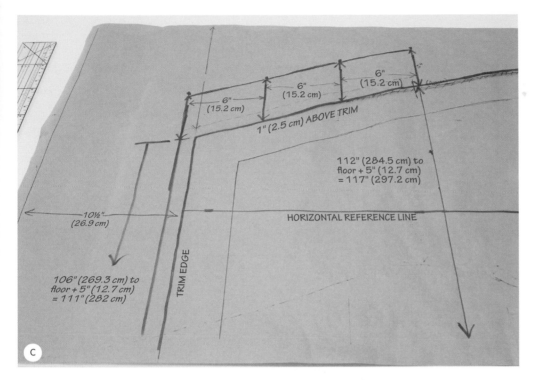

6" (15.2 cm)

6" (15.2 cm)

6" (15.2 cm)

1" (2.5 cm) ABOVE TRIM

112" (284.5 cm) to floor + 5" (12.7 cm) = 117" (297.2 cm)

HORIZONTAL REFERENCE LINE

10½" (26.9 cm)

TRIM EDGE

106" (269.3 cm) to floor + 5" (12.7 cm) = 111" (282 cm)

C

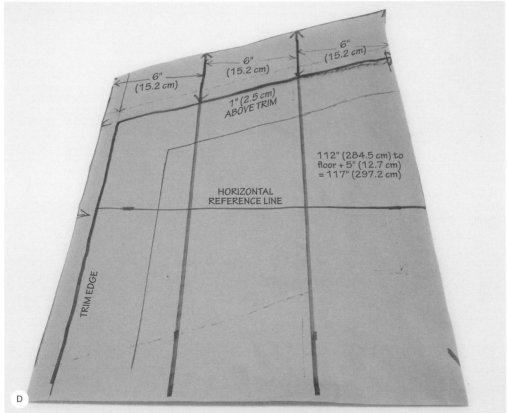

6" (15.2 cm)

6" (15.2 cm)

6" (15.2 cm)

1" (2.5 cm) ABOVE TRIM

112" (284.5 cm) to floor + 5" (12.7 cm) = 117" (297.2 cm)

HORIZONTAL REFERENCE LINE

TRIM EDGE

D

8. Cut apart the pattern on the vertical "pleat" lines. **(E)**

9. Cut strips of paper the size of the pleats. For this curtain, the pleats are 7 inches (17.8 cm) across. Enlarge the pattern by adding the pleat sections. On the front edge add a small space and side hem and on the opposite side a side hem and return. **(F)**

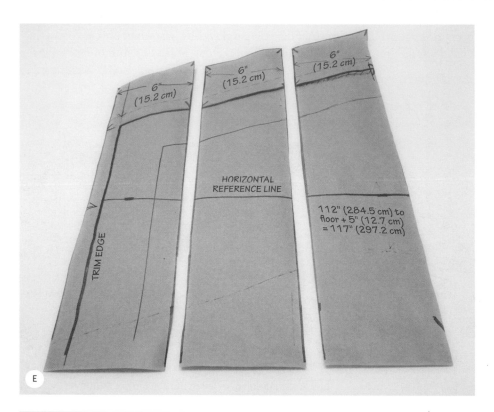

E

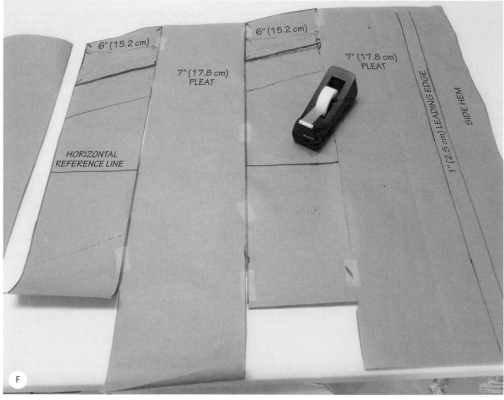

F

10. Connect the horizontal reference line across the pattern and cut the bottom even. This is the pattern you would use for an arched curtain with plain, flat spaces. **(G)**

11. Cut the pattern apart in the center of each space and add enough paper to make the spaces the size measured previously. For this curtain each space is enlarged 4½ inches (11.4 cm). **(H)**

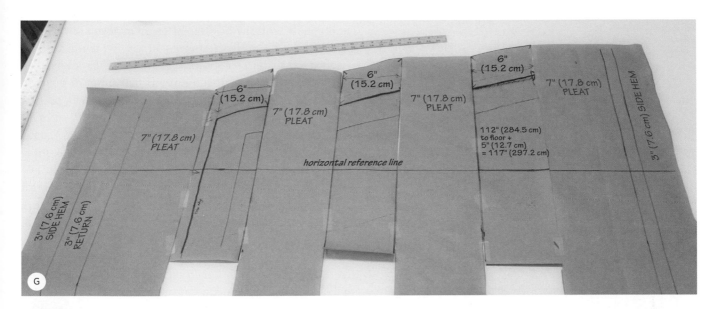

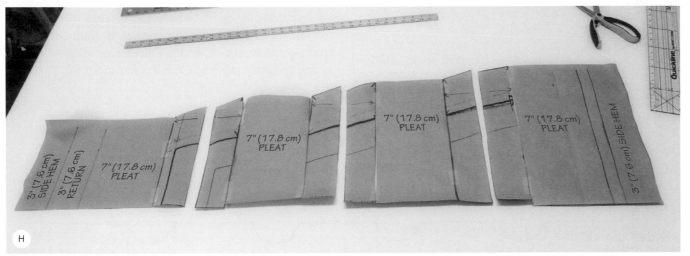

Making Arched Panels on Medallions

1. Seam together the face fabric and lining.

2. With the fabric right side up, place the paper pattern at the top, using the reference line to square the pattern on the fabric. If room allows, adjust the pattern left or right to place seams so they are hidden behind pleats. Add a ½-inch (1.3 cm) seam allowance across the top of the pattern and cut to shape. Use this to cut the opposite side by placing the two curtain panels face-to-face, lining up the seams, matching the pattern motif and cutting to match. (A)

3. Cut the lining the same as the face fabric. A facing is applied to the lining at the top to prevent the lining from showing. Cut the facing out of matching fabric using the pattern and adding a ½-inch (1.3 cm) seam allowance at the top. (B)

4. Drop the pattern down 5 inches (12.7 cm) and cut to create a shaped strip. Cut one more to create an opposite for the other panel. Press ½ inch (1.3 cm) under along the bottom edge of the facings, clipping curves as needed. Attach the facings with fabric glue to the outside top of the linings, matching up the shaped top edge. (C)

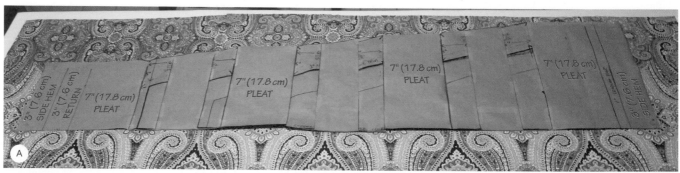

Use the pattern to cut the face fabric. Add a ½-inch (1.3 cm) seam allowance across the top edge when cutting.

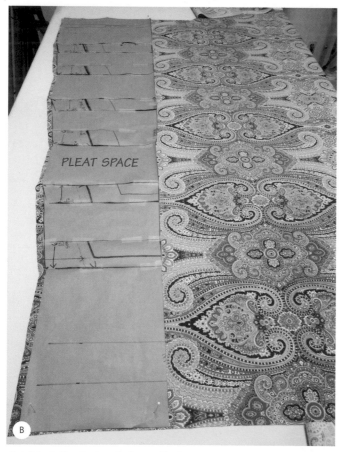

Cut fabric for the top facing to fit the top.

Turn under the bottom edge of the facing and attach to the lining with fabric glue.

5. Place the lining with facing attached face up and top with the matching face piece, face down. Line up the shaped top and pin together. Sew across the top using a ½-inch (1.3 cm) seam allowance and repeat for the opposite curtain panel. (D)

6. Clip curves and corners and turn the curtains right sides out. Press the seam along the top edges. (E)

7. Straighten and smooth the curtain panel with the lining and face fabric neat and square. Place the pattern at the top and use the reference line to measure across the panel. Use the measurements taken at the window to determine the length from the line. This is much more accurate than measuring the shaped top.

8. Measure from the reference line to the bottom, allowing 8 inches (20.3 cm) for the bottom hem in the face fabric. Fold and press a 4-inch (10.2 cm) doubled hem and pin. The lining will be 1 inch (2.5 cm) shorter with a 3-inch (7.6 cm) doubled hem. Finish the hems. Fold and press the side hems and finish. The panel is ready to be pleated.

D

Pin together the lining and front pieces across the top and sew together.

E

Press the seam at the top.

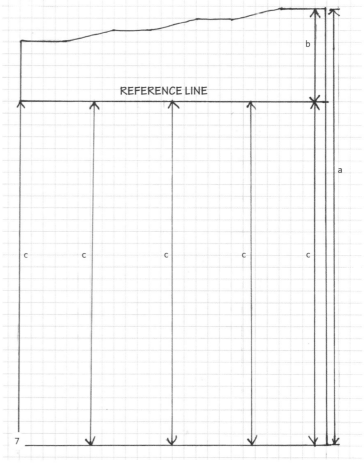

Measure the length.
a. Length at the longest point
b. Measurement from the top edge to the reference line
c. a - b = length used to measure from the reference line

F

Make tabs to fit the medallions.

9. For this curtain, tabs were used to loop over the post of each medallion. This works perfectly for medallions that have a removable front piece. For medallions that have a fixed front piece, add two ties at each pleat, which can be tied over the post. Cut the tabs four times the finished width by the length needed. Fold in half, and then in half again, and topstitch. Set the tabs aside until needed. **(F)**

10. Use the pattern to mark pleats with pins. **(G)** Fold each pleat pin-to-pin and sew 4 inches (10.2 cm) from the top down. **(H)** Be careful to sew the pleats square; it can be confusing because of the uneven top edge. Sew tabs on the inside back of each pleat **(I)** and tack the tops by hand stitching. **(J)**

PLEAT SPACE

G

Use the pattern to mark pleats.

Fold the pleats and pin. Sew from the top down 4 inches (10.2 cm).

Machine stitch the tabs on the inside of each pleat at the back.

Pinch the pleats at the top into three folds and stitch together.

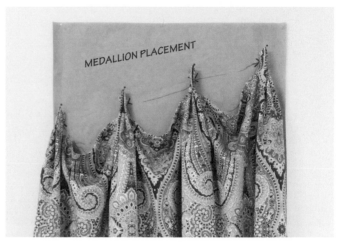

Test the finished curtain on the template made earlier.

Mount the medallions to the wall using the template to mark the spacing.

Loop the tabs over the posts and attach the front pieces. Dress the curtains by pulling the spaces forward at the top, creating a pretty draped effect.

SHADES AND BLINDS

There are many styles of shades: Roman, balloon, London, and more. Even though they have completely different looks, they all share one similarity. Shades operate vertically, raised up and lowered down, instead of traversing across the window like curtains. This offers more design options for your windows.

Shades and blinds are commonly paired with curtains for complete coverage of the window. A superior window covering for insulating the window and because they can be made with a small projection, they are a good choice for inside mounting and layering.

Even though styles like Roman shades are very useful, many times shades are purely decorative and set in a fixed position, especially balloon and London shades, which require dressing.

Roman Shades

Roman shades are made from flat panels of fabric with rings sewn to the back in columns. Cord is threaded through the rings, and when pulled, the fabric is lifted into even, horizontal folds. Once you learn the basic steps, other shades will be easy to accomplish. Choose stable home décor fabrics that do not stretch and preshrink fabrics by pressing with a steam iron prior to cutting and sewing. Roman shades can be functional and lifted up and down, but because they require cords you will want to familiarize yourself with important cord safety information found in Chapter 3: Fundamental Techniques. Best practice is to use only cord-free window treatments in homes with small children.

The basic, flat Roman shade is simple in style, and simple to make.

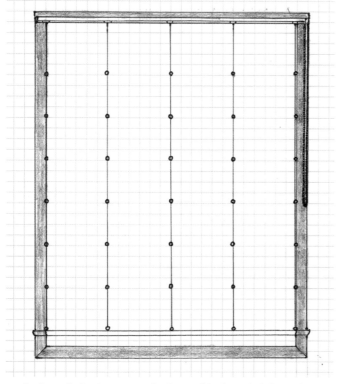

Back view of a basic Roman shade. Cord is threaded through columns of rings and into the lifting system.

BASIC ROMAN SHADE

Roman shades are made from flat panels of fabric with rings sewn to the back in columns. Cord is threaded through the rings and when it is pulled, the fabric is lifted into even, horizontal folds. Shades made today use safety products and cord shrouds to control hazardous cord loops. Once you learn the basic steps, other shades will be easy to accomplish.

Shade rings are available in metal or plastic. They all perform the same so you can select the style you prefer. If using plastic rings, make sure they are UV stable and designed for use on window treatments.

Nylon lift cord is available in different diameters such as 0.9 mm or 1.4 mm. Some shade systems require a specific size of cord. You can also purchase nylon-braided cord (also called "line") in the cord and rope aisle of your local home improvement store.

To meet safety standards, special products such a cord shrouds and RingLocks are used on the back of the shade to control how far the cord can be pulled away from the fabric, making it safer because the size of the combined loop of fabric and cord is minimized. Most cord control products are interchangeable with different lift systems but check with the supplier first to see if there are special requirements. You will see different options used for the projects in this section.

Getting Started

There are a wide variety of systems used for operating blinds and shades, from tracks with interior spools to roller tubes with a clutch, spring, or motors. No matter which system you use, the process for making a basic shade applies, but it's a good idea to purchase the system first, to determine if any special processes or supplies are needed.

When mounting Roman shades on the wall outside of the window frame or opening, plan to extend 1 inch (2.5 cm) beyond each side of the window and several inches above if you can, to expose more window view when the shade is lifted. For inside-mounted Roman shades, allow ¼ inch (6 mm) clearance on each side.

An assortment of shade rings in metal and plastic.

Shade cord is woven in and out of a cord shroud to prevent it from being pulled away from the back of the shade.

An example of two different lifting systems: track with interior spools and roller tube.

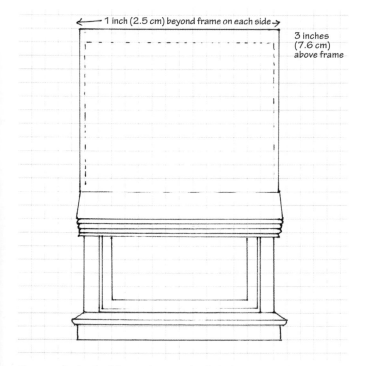

← 1 inch (2.5 cm) beyond frame on each side →

3 inches (7.6 cm) above frame

Roman shades look best when made slightly wider and several inches taller than the window.

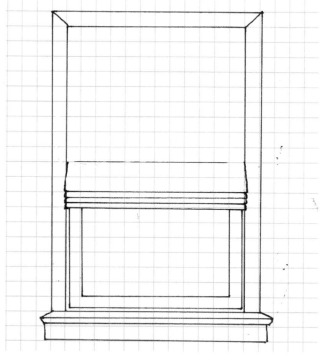

A Roman shade mounted inside the window opening.

What You Will Need

- decorator fabric
- lining
- mounting board
- metal rod or wooden dowel
- heavy-duty stapler and staples
- sew-on Roman shade rings
- Safe-T-Shade RingLocks or cord shroud
- shade cord
- cord adjusting orbs
- lifting system
- tools and hardware for installation

Yardage Requirements

To determine yardage, add allowances to the finished size as outlined below.

MAIN FABRIC

Measure your window and determine the finished width and length of your shade.

A. Finished length of shade ____ + 6 inches (15.2 cm) = _____ ÷ 36 inches (91.4 cm) = _____ yards (meters) of fabric

B. Finished width ____ + 8 inches (20.3 cm) = _____ ÷ fabric width = _____. If this number is greater than 1, double the amount from Step A.

If using more than one width of a print fabric, you may need to match the pattern motif, which could require additional fabric.

Finished length of shade = ____ + 6 inches (15.2 cm) = _____ ÷ pattern repeat = _____ (round up). This is how many of pattern repeats you will need for each cut.

Pattern repeat ____ x number of pattern repeats needed ÷ 36 inches (91.4 cm) = _____ yards (meters)

LINING FABRIC

A. Finished length of shade ____ + 2 inches (5 cm) = _____ ÷ 36 inches (91.4 cm) = _____ yards (meters)

B. Finished shade width = _____ ÷ fabric width = _____. If this number is greater than 1, double the amount from Step A.

When sewing multiple widths together, you may want to split widths in half lengthwise for a whole piece in the center, with sew half widths to each side. Study the pattern motif to determine what is best. For shades with a short length, you can railroad fabrics and linings. This will allow you to have a wide shade without any seams.

Making a Basic Roman Shade

1. Cut the main fabric the finished width plus 8 inches (20.3 cm) wide and the finished length plus 6 inches (15.2 cm) long. For a large shade, seam together the fabric cuts and press seams open before cutting to size.

2. Place the main fabric face down, and fold over 4 inches (10.2 cm) along one side, iron in a crease, and then fold the cut edge under and press, creating a 2-inch (5 cm) doubled hem. Repeat for the other side and bottom hem, double-checking the measurement across the width of the shade.

3. At the bottom left and right corners, sew a mitered seam. This is optional; you can leave the bottom corners square. To create the mitered corner seam, unfold the pressed hems and measure 6 inches (15.2 cm) from the edge on one corner, making a mark at the center of the fold. (A) Draw a line from the inside corner to the outer corner, creating a right angle. (B) Fold the corner on the bias, pin, and stitch on the line. (C) Trim off excess fabric (D), turn right sides out, and press. (E)

A

Unfold the pressed hems at the corner. You will see the creases from pressing the hems. Measure 6 inches (15.2 cm) from the edge and mark in the center of the hem.

B

Draw a line, creating a right angle from the inside corner to the mark and out to the edge.

C

Fold the corner on the bias, lining up the cut edges and pinning together. Sew on the marked line.

D

Cut off excess fabric.

E

Turn right sides out and press.

The finished corner is neat and has less bulk than the double-folded square corner.

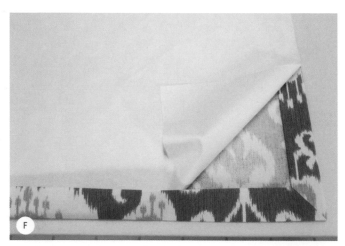

Cut the lining to the exact finished width and place it under the hems.

A rod pocket is sewn above the bottom hem.

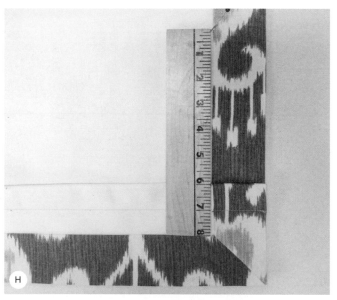

Mark 7 inches (17.8 cm) from the rod pocket stitch line and then continue marking every 8 inches (20.3 cm) to the top of the shade.

4. Place the hemmed fabric face down and top with the lining face up, smoothing it out neatly. Trim off excess lining even with the side and bottom edges and tuck the edges under the hems. Secure the hems with pins. Hand sew the hems around all three sides or finish using your preferred method. (See Chapter 3: Fundamental Techniques.) Secure the top edge with pins. (F)

5. With the shade face down, fold over 4 inches (10.2 cm) at the bottom and press. Draw a line 1 inch (2.5 cm) from the folded edge, pin, and straight stitch to create a rod pocket. (G)

6. Mark for the rings on the back of the shade. Begin with the vertical spacing by measuring along the inside edge of the side hem, beginning at the rod pocket stitch line and measuring 7 inches (17.8 cm). Make a small mark on the lining next to the side hem. Measure from that mark up toward the top, spacing marks 8 inches (20.3 cm) apart, until you are within 12 inches (20.3 cm) or less of the finished length. Repeat for the opposite side. This will create 4-inch (10.2 cm) folds as the shade is lifted. You can adjust the vertical spacing. For example, if using 3-inch (7.6 cm) folds with the rings spaced 6 inches (15.2 cm) apart vertically, subtract 1 inch (2.5 cm) from the instructions above. (H)

7. Next, mark for horizontal spacing of the rings across the shade. Measure between the outer marks at the side hems and divide by a number that will result in 9 inches (22.9 cm) or less. Mark across the top edge of the rod pocket and continue from the bottom to the top marks. (I)

8. Pin together the face fabric and lining at each mark to hold the layers together. Sew a shade ring at each mark using a thread to match the face, sewing all the way through to the front and removing the pins. Rings can be hand sewn or machine sewn using a button-sewing attachment. The rings should be sewn so that they are parallel with the top and bottom. Make sure the bottom rings sewn to the rod pocket are secure, as they will bear the weight of the shade. (J)

9. Cut a metal rod or wooden dowel 1 inch (2.5 cm) less than the finished width and insert inside the rod pocket. Sew or glue the ends of the pocket closed. (K)

Create a template for ring spacing on a straight edge or ruler with marked pieces of tape. Move the template from row to row. This will save time!

Make sure the bottom rings sewn to the rod pocket are secure, as they will bear the weight of the shade.

A painted steel rod is needed for some lift systems. The extra weight creates tension needed for the system to engage. Otherwise, an aluminum rod or wooden dowel will work just fine.

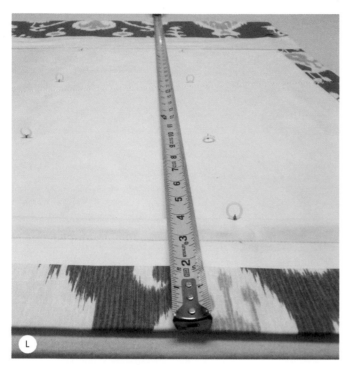

For the most accurate length, measure after the rings are sewn and the rod is inserted in the pocket.

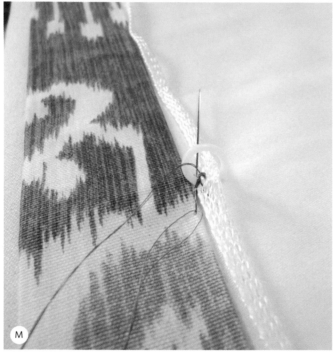

Sew the cord shroud at each ring. Do not stitch over the cord within.

10. With the shade face down, measure from the bottom to the top, folding over at the finished length and pressing to create a crease. Cut off excess fabric, allowing for 2 inches (5 cm) past the crease line for attaching to the board. (L)

This shade uses a cord shroud tube to meet safety standards. The tube is stitched in place at each ring. (M) You can sew rings and shroud all at the same time. Tie-off the shroud to the top and bottom rings. The cord within the tube is fished out at the bottom and fastened with a cord-adjusting orb. (N) At the top ring, the cord is fished out of the shroud tube and threaded into the lifting system.

Note: Some cord shrouds are made without the cord and you will thread the cord into the shroud.

11. Cut the board to the finished width. Cover the ends of the board with the face fabric. Draw a line on top of the board 2 inches (5 cm) from the edge and staple the shade to the board at the line. Continue covering the board, hiding cut edges and staples. (See page 196.)

12. Attach the shade lifting system to the board and thread the cords into the system.

13. Install the shade to the wall using angle irons or the brackets supplied with the lifting system. (See Chapter 7: Installing Window Treatments.) Some fabrics require training to fall into neat folds. To do this, pull the shade to the highest position and steam. Smooth over the fabrics, creasing with your hands along the horizontal folds.

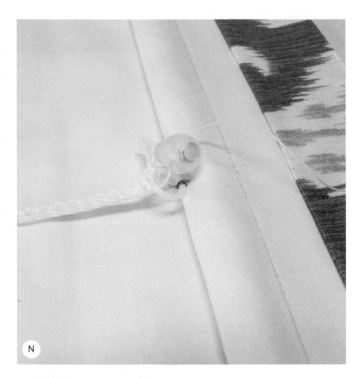

Fish the cord from the shroud and secure with an orb.

Cords run from the bottom to the top within the shroud, lifting the shade.

BLACKOUT ROMAN SHADE WITH RIBS

When making Roman shades in the usual way, there is stitching to the front where the rings are sewn. This is an important step because it connects the face fabric to the rings so that the shade folds up evenly when it is lifted. When blackout lining is used, the holes created when sewing the rings make pinholes of light when the sun is shining. This can be very distracting, and a disappointment after so much work sewing a custom shade. This project will show you how to avoid this problem.

This shade is made with ribs for even folds when lifted and blackout lining for light control.

Getting Started

With this method, the interlining is attached to the face fabric first and then the blackout lining is sewn with the rings to the back of the rib pockets. The extra steps are worth it! You'll be pleased with the expert quality of the finished shade and there will be no pesky pinholes of light!

What You Will Need

- decorator fabric
- flannel interlining
- blackout lining
- plastic shade ribs
- sew-on Roman shade rings
- shade cord and cord shroud
- cord-adjusting orbs
- mounting board
- heavy-duty stapler and staples
- lifting system
- Flat aluminium bar (1 inch [2.5 cm])
- tools and hardware for installation

Yardage Requirements

Roman shades are a flat style of window treatment without any fullness. To determine yardage, add allowances to the finished size as outlined below.

MAIN FABRIC

Measure your window and determine the finished width and length of your shade.

A. Finished length of shade ____ + 6 inches (15.2 cm) = _____ ÷ 36 inches (91.4 cm) = _____ yards (meters) of fabric

B. Finished width ____ + 8 inches (20.3 cm) = _____ ÷ fabric width = _____. If this number is greater than 1, double the amount from Step A.

If using more than one width of a print fabric, you may need to match the pattern motif, which could require additional fabric.

Finished length of shade = ____ + 6 inches (15.2 cm) = _____ ÷ pattern repeat = _____ (round up)

This is how many pattern repeats you will need for each cut.

Pattern repeat ____ x number of pattern repeats needed ÷ 36 inches (91.4 cm) = _____ yards (meters)

LINING FABRIC

A. Finished length of shade ____ + 2 inches (5 cm) = _____ ÷ 36 inches (91.4 cm) = _____ yards (meters)

B. Finished shade width = _____ ÷ fabric width = _____. If this number is greater than 1, double the amount from Step A.

INTERLINING FABRIC

A. Finished length of shade ____ + 4 inches (10.2 cm) for every 12 inches (30.5 cm) of length ÷ 36 inches (91.4 cm) = _____ yards (meters). For example, if the shade is finished 60 inches (152.4 cm) long, add 20 inches (50.8 cm).

When sewing multiple widths together, you may want to split widths in half lengthwise for a whole piece in the center, and sew half widths to each side. Study the pattern motif to determine what is best. For shades with a short length, you can railroad fabrics and linings. This will allow you to have a wide shade without any seams.

Making a Blackout Roman Shade with Ribs

1. Follow instructions for making a basic Roman shade, to the point of adding the lining.

2. Cut the interlining a few inches (7.6 cm) wider than the finished width. For the length, allow 4 inches (10.2 cm) extra per 12 inches (30.5 cm) of length. Starting at the bottom, measure and sew rib pockets across the width of the interlining. The spacing between the pockets should be 8 inches (20.3 cm) or less. Choose the best spacing for your fabric and finished length.

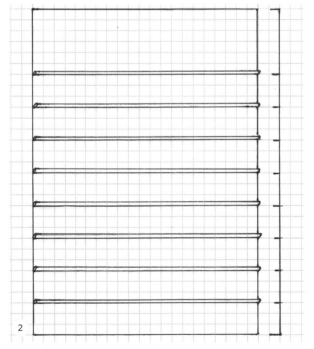

Rib pockets are spaced equally from the bottom to the top.

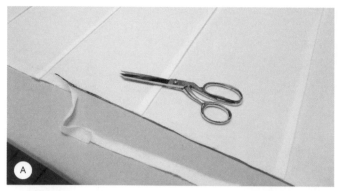

Cut off excess interlining even and square to fit the shade.

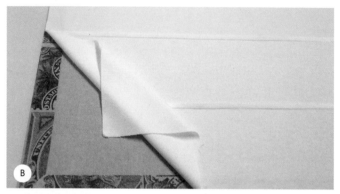

With the shade face down, place the interlining over the back with rib pockets facing up.

Pin the interlining to the back of the face fabric, under each rib pocket.

Sew the interlining to the face fabric under each rib pocket with a small stitch spaced 5 to 6 inches (12.7 to 15.2 cm) apart. Knot the thread before moving to the next stitch.

3. The first pocket should be sewn above the bottom edge, half the size of the rib spacing. If using 8-inch (20.3 cm) spacing, the first rib pocket will be 4 inches (10.2 cm) above the bottom. This will allow the bottom edge of the shade to be even with the folds. This can be adjusted if you want more of the hem to show. For this shade, the first rib pocket was sewn 8 inches (20.3 cm) from the bottom, to allow the bottom hem and trim to show. Make a muslin template if you are unsure of the spacing, before cutting fabrics.

4. Measure the circumference of the plastic rib to determine what size to make the pockets. You do not want the pockets to be too tight. This shade used ½-inch (1.3 cm) pockets. Sew the first rib pocket by folding over the fabric, measuring, pressing a crease, and pinning together. Draw a line, or mark the machine with blue low-tack tape for sewing an even seam.

5. After the first pocket is sewn, measure to the next rib pocket and continue sewing. Make sure all rib pockets are sewn on the same side of the interlining. After all the pockets are sewn, iron the entire piece, pressing the pockets all facing toward the top. (A)

6. Place the shade with pressed hems face down and place the interlining with rib pockets evenly over the back. Line up the bottom edge of the interlining with the bottom of the shade. Smooth the interlining neatly in place. Measure to make sure the rib pockets are even and square. (B)

7. Cut off the side edges of the interlining even with the shade. Tuck the interlining under the hems on all three sides. Add pins horizontally under the rib pockets. (C)

8. Secure the interlining to the face fabric by hand sewing under each rib pocket. (D) Use strong thread, matching the color to the face fabric. Starting at the side hem, make a stitch through the interlining to the front and back out, secure the thread with a stitched knot (E), and then continue across to make another small stitch under the rib pocket. Space the stitches about a hand's width apart. You do not need to line up the stitches in rows or clip the threads between each stitch.

9. Continue sewing the interlining to the face fabric under each rib pocket. After the hand stitching is completed, add the ribs.

10. Cut the plastic ribs 1 inch (2.5 cm) less than the finished width. Fold back the side hem and slide the ribs into the pockets. (F) (G)

11. Cover the back with blackout lining. You can precut the lining to the finished size, or place a larger piece over the back and cut to fit. Tuck the blackout under the bottom and side hems. Pin the hems for hand sewing.

12. Mark for placement of the shade rings on the back of each rib pocket in even columns, 9 to 12 inches (22.9 to 30.5 cm) apart horizontally. (H)

13. Hand tack shade rings to the back at each mark. The stitching will be on top of a rib pocket, catching the blackout lining and interlining over the plastic rib. (I)

Stitch a secure knot on the back at each tack point.

Slide a plastic rib into each pocket.

The ribs are in place.

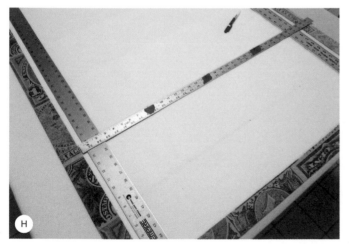

Mark for the shade rings on top of each rib pocket.

Sew shade rings to the back of the shade, over each rib.

Place a flat aluminum bar in the bottom hem.

Sew the hems, catching the lining and interlining only.

Measure, fold, and press at the finished length.

Apply trim across the bottom hem. Low-tack tape marks the spacing.

14. Cut a flat aluminum bar 1 inch (2.5 cm) less than the finished width and place it in the bottom hem. Hand sew the side and bottom hems. (J)

15. Sew the side and bottom hems, catching the blackout lining and interlining but not stitching all the way through to the front. (K)

16. Measure from the bottom to the top, folding over excess fabric and marking for the finished length. Leave extra at the top for board mounting. (L)

17. Cut the mounting board and attach the shade, finishing the board neatly. (See Chapter 7: Installing Window Treatments.)

Making Optional Return End Flaps

This shade has small flaps to cover the ends of the board and hide the lifting system. Cut the fabric and blackout lining to the size needed for your board and lifting system. Allow at least 2 inches (5 cm) to wrap to the front. Add 2 inches (5 cm) to the bottom edge for the hem.

1. With the fabrics face-to-face, sew a 1-inch (2.5 cm) seam along the bottom. (A)

2. Turn over the face fabric so that it is doubled on the bottom edge. Pin and sew each side edge with a ½-inch (1.3 cm) seam allowance. (B)

3. Turn right sides out and press. Add an iron-on stiffener like buckram or heavy interfacing inside, to keep the end flaps neat. (C)

4. Turn over the top edges and hand sew loop strip to the back.

5. Staple the hook tape to the board and attach. This makes it easy when installing to remove the flaps and then put them back in place. (D)

6. Continue to finish the shade by attaching the lifting system and cord shrouds or RingLocks to control hazardous cord loops. Use cord-adjusting orbs at the bottom of the shade for adjusting the length.

7. The shade is completed and ready to install over the window.

Return end flaps hide the end of the board and the lifting system.

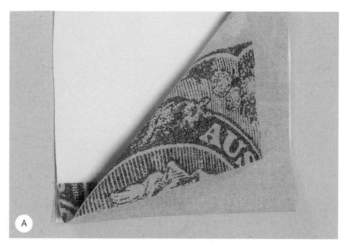

Sew across the bottom with a 1-inch (2.5 cm) seam. Turn over the fabric so it is doubled on the bottom.

Sew each side and clip the corners.

Press the flaps and add buckram or interfacing to stiffen.

Attach the end return flaps to the face edge of the board with hook-and-loop tape.

Even on bright, sunny days there will not be pinholes of light on this blackout shade.

RELAXED ROMAN SHADE

A relaxed Roman shade is less structured and has a softer look than a flat shade. The objective is to add a small amount of fullness, providing enough ease for the bottom hem to swag slightly. This can be achieved in several ways: by cutting the shade with a flared bottom section, by adding small pleats to each end, by adding one pleat in the center, or by angling the rings wider at the bottom.

Getting Started

In this instruction you will learn how to make a relaxed shade by cutting the bottom wider, in a fishtail shape. This is one of the easiest shades to make! These shades are non-working and set in a fixed position. Boards with Velcro are used to make installation easy. Stationary shades like this are the perfect choice for children's rooms—there are no hazardous cords and they are easy to remove for cleaning.

If you would like the shade to be operable, this method is a good choice because the body of the shade is made straight and square; only the bottom section is shaped. The shade will stack up into neat folds above the relaxed hem.

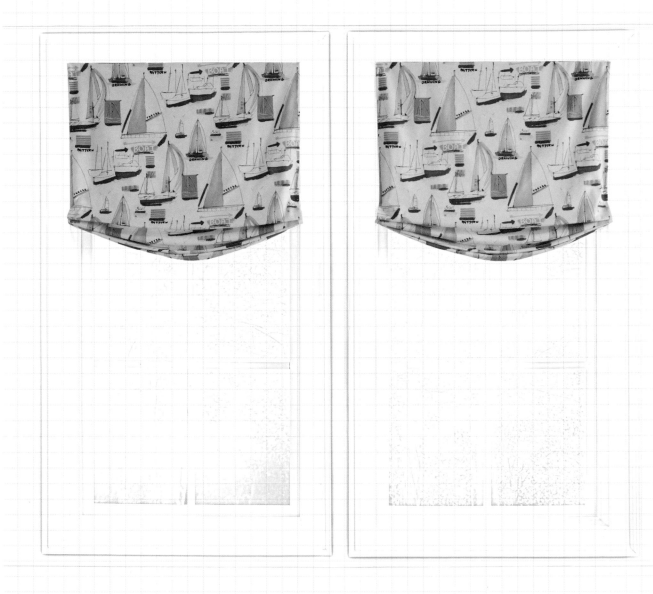

This version of a Roman shade has soft folds at the bottom hem.

What You Will Need

- decorator fabric
- lining
- mounting board
- wooden dowel
- ¾-inch (1.8 cm) sew-on Velcro (hook and loop)
- heavy-duty stapler and staples
- small cable ties
- sew-on Roman shade rings
- tools and hardware for installation

Yardage Requirements

MAIN FABRIC

Measure your window and determine the finished width and length of your shade.

A. Finished length of shade ____ + 20½ inches (21.6 cm) = _____ ÷ 36 inches (91.4cm) = _____ yards (meters) of fabric

B. Finished width _____ + 4 inches (10.2 cm) = _____ ÷ fabric width = _____. If this number is greater than 1, double the amount from Step A.

If using more than one width of a print fabric, you may need to match the pattern motif, which could require additional fabric.

Finished length of shade = ____ + 20½ inches (21.6 cm) = _____ ÷ pattern repeat = _____ (round up). This is how many of pattern repeats you will need for each cut.

Pattern repeat ____ x number of pattern repeats needed ÷ 36 inches (91.4cm) = _____ yards (meters)

LINING FABRIC

A. Finished length of shade ____ + 20½ inches (21.6 cm) = _____ ÷ 36 inches (91.4cm) = _____ yards (meters)

B. Finished shade width = _____ + 4 inches (10.2 cm) ÷ fabric width = _____. If this number is greater than 1, double the amount from Step A.

When sewing multiple widths together, you may want to split widths in half lengthwise for a whole piece in the center, and sew half widths to each side. Study the pattern motif to determine what is best. For shades with a short length, you can railroad fabrics and linings. This will allow you to have a wide shade without any seams.

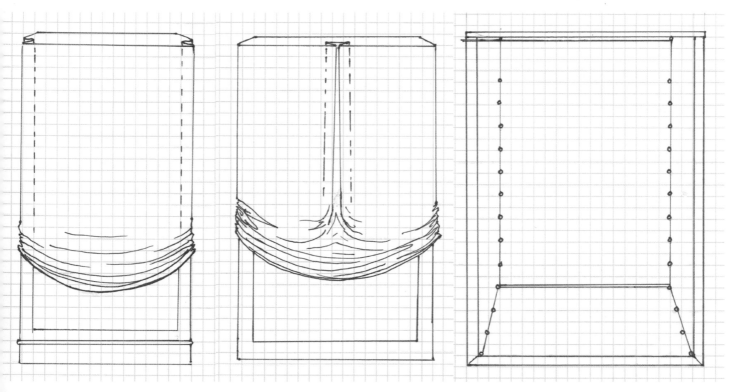

Small pleats are added at each side to create the fullness needed for the relaxed, swag bottom hem.

One pleat can be used in the center to create a relaxed shade. Use minimal fullness; too large of a pleat will make the shade droop and look baggy in the center.

Back view of a Roman shade with rings angled wider at the bottom to create a relaxed style. The weight bar matches the width of the rings in the body of the shade.

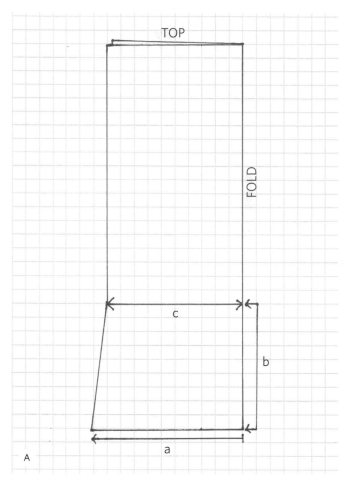

The fabric is folded and marked so that the bottom section is wider than the main body of the shade.

Press from the front, making sure the lining doesn't peek out from behind the edges.

Making a Relaxed Roman Shade

1. Measure the window to determine the finished width. For an inside-mounted shade, deduct ¼ inch (6 mm). Measure an approximate finished length; it can be adjusted later.

2. Fold the fabric lengthwise, right sides together. Starting at the bottom, measure and mark as shown in the diagram (a) half the finished width plus 2 inches (5 cm), (b) 18½ inches (47 cm), and (c) half the finished width plus 1 inch (2.5 cm), which will continue to the top. Cut and unfold. (A)

3. Place the lining face up and top with the cut face fabric, face down. Cut the lining to fit and pin to hold the edges together. Sew the side and bottom edges using a ½-inch (1.3 cm) seam allowance.

4. Turn right sides out and press the front and back, making sure the edges are flat and neat. (B)

5. Place the shade face down and mark ring placement from the bottom, 1 inch (2.5 cm) from the edge and 6 inches (15.2 cm) apart. Continue to the height needed for a stationary shade, or to within 12 inches (30.5 cm) of the finished length for a working shade. Repeat for the opposite side.

6. Sew shade rings at each mark, catching the face fabric with the stitches. (C)

7. Measure from the bottom to the top and mark at the finished length plus ¾ inch (1.8 cm). Cut away any excess fabric. On the front top edge, pin Velcro loop strip and machine sew to the shade. (D) Fold over and hand sew the Velcro to the back. (E) You can also machine sew, but the stitches will show from the front.

8. Cut a wooden dowel 2 inches (5 cm) less than the finished width and cover with a sleeve of lining and hand sew above the rings at the top of the angled bottom section. This will keep the shade from pulling in at the sides. (F)

9. Cinch together the four shade rings at the bottom section, plus additional rings up the side to achieve the desired length using a small cable tie. If making a working shade, cinch together only the bottom four rings to create stationary folds. (G)

10. Cut the board to the finished width. Cover with lining and staple Velcro hook strip to the front. Install the board at the window and attach the shade. (See Chapter 7: Installing Window Treatments.) Smooth the folds at the bottom of the shade so that they hang evenly.

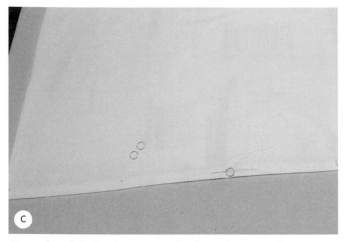

On a relaxed shade, rings are used only on the outer edges.

Velcro loop strip is pinned and then machine sewn to the front.

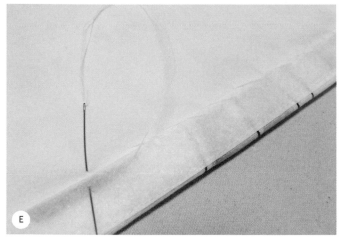

The Velcro is folded under to the reverse side and secured with hand sewing. Do not catch the face fabric with the stitches.

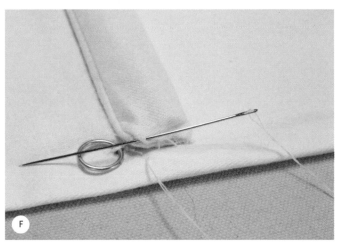

A fabric-covered dowel is sewn to the outside edges to keep the shade from pulling in on each side.

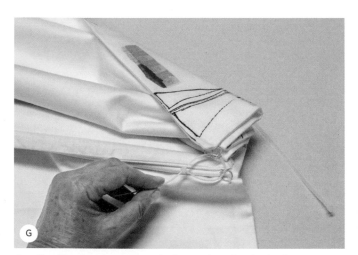

Small cable ties are used to cinch together the shade rings on each side.

Cut off excess cable tie. The shade is ready to install.

BALLOON SHADE

This style of shade is made with softly gathered fabric, which falls off thc top of the board and then is lifted up from the bottom with cords. Also known as "cloud shades," balloon shades have a soft, unstructured appearance. Choose soft fabrics and linings to keep the shades from being weighted down. Balloon shades can be functional and lifted up and down, but because they require dressing to neaten them, it is more practical to make them set in a fixed position.

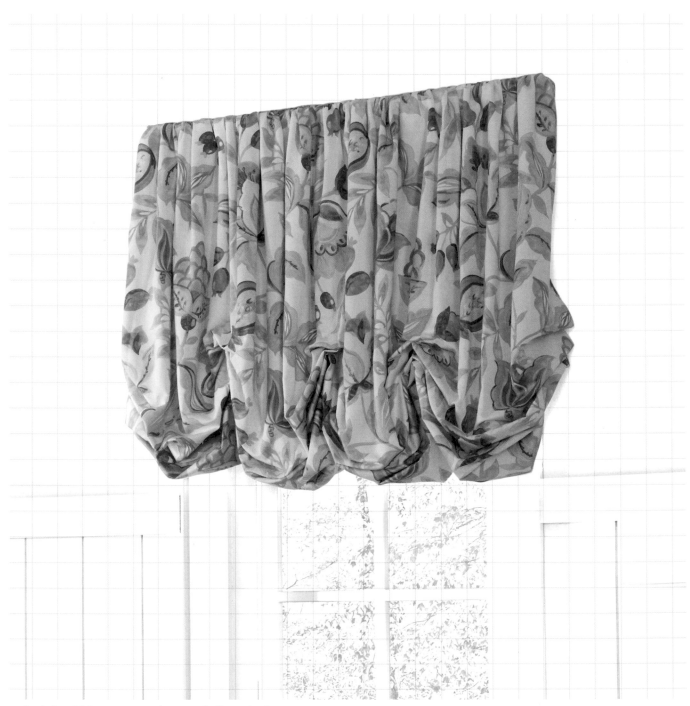

A fresh floral fabric creates a feminine balloon shade.

Getting Started

Plan to mount the board above the window frame and 1 inch (2.5 cm) beyond the frame on the sides. As with other shades, mount several inches above the window if you can, to expose more window view.

What You Will Need

- decorator fabric
- lining
- mounting board cut to size
- heavy-duty stapler and staples
- tools and hardware for installation
- screw eyes
- sew-on Roman shade rings
- Safe-T-Shade RingLocks or cord shroud
- shade cord
- cord-adjusting orb

Yardage Requirements

To determine the number of cuts or widths, measure across the mounting board and around each end and multiple times the desired fullness, such as two or two and a half, and divide by the fabric width. (See Chapter 3: Fundamental Techniques.) It is not recommended to make balloon shades with more than two and a half times fullness unless it is an unlined, thin material.

Board measurement x fullness ÷ fabric width = number of cuts needed (round up)

To determine the cut length, measure to where you would like the longest point to be and add 22 inches (55.9 cm). The finished length is adjustable after the shade is installed.

If using a print fabric, additional fabric may be needed to match the pattern motif.

Cut length x number of cuts needed ÷ 36 inches (91.4 cm) = number of yards (meters) (round up)

Use this calculation to cut lining fabric.

FIGURING YARDAGE FOR FABRICS WITH A PATTERN MOTIF
(SEE CHAPTER 3: FUNDAMENTAL TECHNIQUES)
Cut length ÷ pattern repeat = number repeats needed per cut (round up)

Number of repeats needed x pattern repeat = cut length

Cut length x number of cuts needed ÷ 36 inches (91.4 cm) = number of yards (meters) (round up)

When sewing multiple widths together, you may want to split widths in half lengthwise for a whole piece in the center, and sew half widths to each side. Study the pattern motif to determine what is best. When possible, you can railroad fabrics and linings. This will create a shade without any seams.

Making a Balloon Shade

1. Cut and seam together the fabric and lining. Press the seams open. Place the lining face up and top with the decorator fabric face down, lining up the seams and bottom edges. Sew across the bottom edge using a 1-inch (2.5 cm) seam allowance. Press the seam to one side, facing toward the face fabric. (A)

2. Turn the fabric right sides out and press the bottom seam with the face fabric wrapping to the back, creating a 1-inch (2.5 cm) hem. (B)

The seam is pressed from the reverse side, flat toward the face fabric.

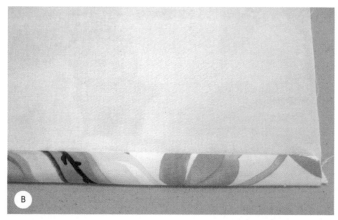

The hem is pressed to reveal 1 inch (2.5 cm) of face fabric on the reverse side.

3. Fold over 3 inches (7.6 cm) on each side. Trim away excess lining and fold under the cut edges to make a 1½-inch (3.8 cm) doubled hem along each side. (C)

4. Press the hems and secure with pins. Finish the side hems by hand or machine sewing or with a fusible hem tape. (D)

5. After the side hems are finished, smooth out the lined fabric and measure and mark the length, remembering to add 2 inches (5 cm) extra at the top for board mounting. Secure with pins and sew across the top with a straight stitch or serged seam.

6. Determine how many poufs, or balloons, you would like on the bottom of the shade by dividing the board width by 10 and rounding up or down. For this shade the finished width was 35 inches (88.9 cm); divided by 10 = 3.5. I rounded up to four balloon poufs across the shade. (E)

7. Place the lined and hemmed shade face down and mark for the columns of rings. There will be rings placed along each side hem with the other rings evenly spaced across the shade. Begin by measuring across the shade from the inside of each side hem and dividing by how many poufs will be used. For example, if the finished flat shade measures 100 inches (254 cm) wide, and four poufs were planned, then each section would be 100 ÷ 4 = 25 inches (63.5 cm) between each column of rings.

8. One quick and easy way to mark a line for the columns of rings is to fold the flat shade lengthwise (into quarters for this example) and press a crease. When you unfold the flat shade fabric, the creases mark where the rings will be sewn. (F)

9. Unfold the shade and make a tiny pencil mark for ring placement starting at the top edge of the bottom hem and up each ironed crease, making the marks 6 inches (15.2 cm) apart. Pin at each mark, catching both the lining and the face fabric. (G)

10. Sew shade rings at each mark, catching the face fabric with the stitches.

11. Cover the mounting board and attach the shade to the top of the board, wrapping around each end and gathering to fit the board as you staple. Finish the top so all of the staples and cut edges are covered. (See Chapter 7: Installing Window Treatments.) (H)

12. Attach small screw eyes under the board and in line with the top ring and 1 inch (2.5 cm) from the shade. Thread the cord through the rings with RingLocks or cord shroud and screw eyes. (See "Cord Safety" in chapter 3.) Cover a wooden dowel or small metal rod with a sleeve of matching fabric and hand stitch it behind the cords, connected to each bottom ring. (I)

13. Install the shade to the wall using angle irons. (See Chapter 7: Installing Window Treatments.) Pull the cord to raise the shade to the desired height and secure the cord by tying off to the last screw eye, or with a cord-adjusting orb. Cut away excess cord and dress the balloon shade with even, soft poufs and gathers.

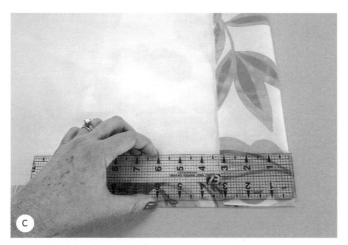

C

Finish the side edges by folding over 3 inches (7.6 cm) and then folding again for a 1½-inch (3.8 cm) finished hem.

D

The doubled side hem is ready to be pinned and finished.

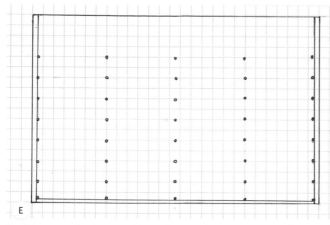

In this example there are five columns of rings to create four poufs on the bottom of the balloon shade.

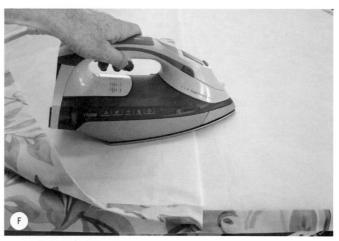

Pressing in a crease is an easy and accurate way to mark vertical ring placement.

Pins are used to mark ring placement and hold fabrics together for sewing.

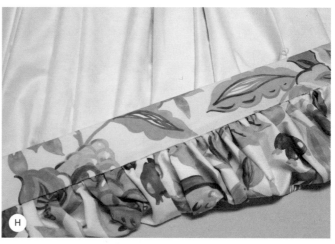

The gathered balloon shade is attached to the top of the board, creating a soft, waterfall of gathers.

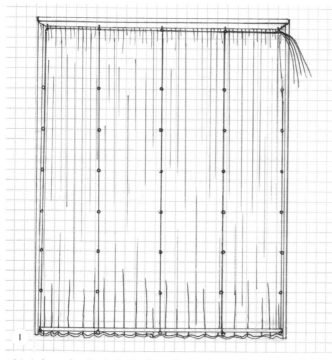

This is how the shade looks from the reverse side. A covered dowel is secured at each bottom ring to keep the sections evenly spaced when the shade is raised.

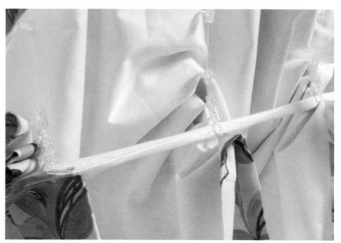

When the shade is raised, the fabric falls between the rings, creating the "poufs" of the balloon shade.

London Shade

London shades are a beautiful style with a traditional flavor. They are best made from light- to medium-weight fabrics. When using printed fabrics, pattern placement is important and must be planned before cutting.

Because London shades cover the top half of the window, it is not a good choice for short windows without room to mount the shade above the frame. Wide windows will require two or more swag sections.

A London shade has pleats inset from each end. When the bottom is lifted, the fabric falls into soft folds in the center with pleated tails on each side

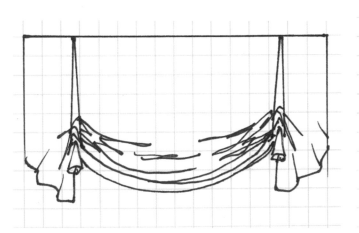

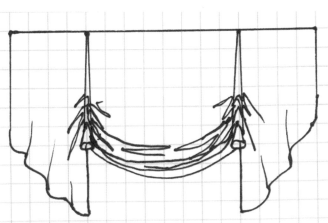

The placement of the pleats determines the length of the tails on the sides. The sketch at left uses a ⅙th proportion while the design on the right has a ¼th proportion.

Getting Started

When designing a London shade, the position of the pleats determines the finished look. The more the pleats are inset from each end, the longer the tails will be and, if you place the pleats close to each end, the tails will be quite short. A good rule of thumb is to divide the finished width by 6 and use that number for spacing the pleats from the outside edges. For example, if the finished width is 42 inches (106.7 cm), divide by 6 for spacing of 7 inches (17.8 cm) from each end. A simple mock-up out of muslin or remnant fabric can help you determine the best proportions for your window.

Do not make the pleats overly full or the center section will have too much volume. A 10-inch (25.4 cm) pleat was used for this project, but a lesser size pleat would have worked with good results.

On a London shade, the side and bottom edges on the reverse should be finished with a matching or complementary fabric so the lining doesn't show. Welt cord or another style of trim can be inserted into the seam.

What You Will Need

- decorator fabric
- lining
- mounting board
- metal rod or wooden dowel
- heavy-duty stapler and staples
- sew-on shade rings
- welt cord
- screw eyes
- shade lift cord
- Safe-T-Shade RingLocks or cord shroud
- cord-adjusting orb (optional)
- tools and hardware for installation

Yardage Requirements

Measure your window and determine the finished width and length of your shade. Because a London shade needs to be dressed after it is installed, it is recommended that it be made stationary. A working London shade would not be practical.

At the window, determine a finished length after the shade is pulled up in position, and add 18 inches (45.7 cm). This is the finished length to be used in the calculations below.

MAIN FABRIC

A. Finished length of shade ____ + 3 inches (7.6 cm) = _____ This is the cut length.

B. Finished width _____ + allowance for pleats _____ + returns _____ + 1 inch (2.5 cm) = _____ ÷ fabric width = _____. This is the number of cuts.

Cut length ____ x number of cuts _____ = ____ ÷ 36 inches (91.4 cm) = ____ yards (meters).

If using more than one width of a print fabric, you may need to match the pattern motif, which could require additional fabric.

Finished length of shade = ____ + 3 inches (7.6 cm) = _____ ÷ pattern repeat = _____ (round up). This is how many of pattern repeats you will need for each cut.

LINING FABRIC

You will need the same amount as the main fabric.

IF RAILROADING THE MAIN FABRIC OR LINING

Finished width _____ + allowance for pleats _____ + returns _____ + 1 inch (2.5 cm) = _____ ÷ 36 inches (91.4 cm) = _____ yards (meters)

Note: Extra fabric will be needed to add a facing around the sides and bottom and welt cord around the edges and along the top of the finished shade.

Making a London Shade

1. Begin by creating a cut plan. The shade has five parts: left, right, center, and two pleats. The left and right pieces include the return, which wraps around the end of the board. Use a strip of paper or fabric to make a template. Mark for seams inside the pleats. (A)

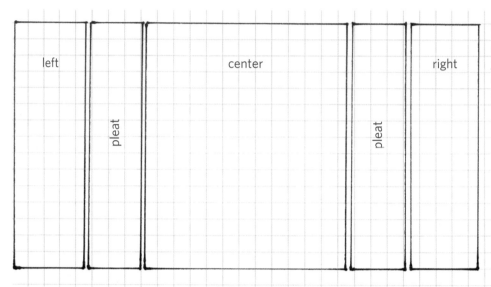

There are five sections for a London shade. If the fabric does not require pattern matching, the sections can be combined, requiring fewer seams.

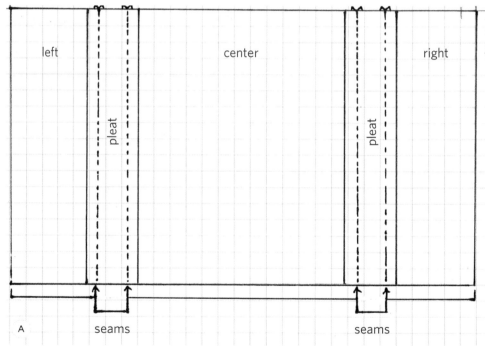

Hide seams inside the pleats. Mark this on the template before cutting fabric.

2. Use the template to determine the cuts, adding ½-inch (1.3 cm) seam allowances. On patterned fabric, make the cuts so that the pattern matches across the shade. **(B)**

3. Sew together the cuts and press the seams open. Cut and sew the lining to match the seamed face fabric. Sew a facing 6 to 8 inches (15.2 to 20.3 cm) wide along the bottom and sides of the lining. **(C)**

4. Cover enough welt cord to go around the sides and bottom edges. Sew the welt cord to the edges of the face fabric. (See Chapter 3: Fundamental Techniques.) **(D)**

5. Pin together the front and back pieces and sew, getting close to the welt cord. Do not sew across the top. **(E)**

6. Trim away the seam allowance to about ¼ inch (6 mm). Turn right sides out and press the edges, checking to make sure the welt cord is sewn neatly. Press on the face and back of the shade. **(F)**

Check cuts before sewing the pieces together to make sure the pattern lines up.

A facing of matching fabric is added around the sides and bottom of the lining. This prevents the lining from showing when the shade is lifted.

Sew welt cord around the edges of the seamed face fabric.

Pin the front and back together face-to-face and sew around the edges.

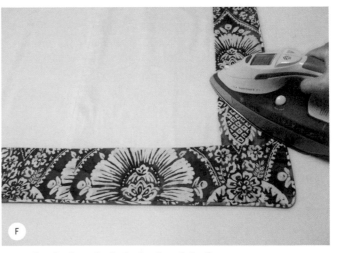

Press the shade on both the back and the front.

7. Measure and mark the length, adding extra for board mounting. Cut off excess fabric and pin the fabrics together across the top.

8. Mark for the pleats and fold them evenly down the length of the shade and press. **(G)** Use pins to hold the pleats flat. **(H)**

9. With the pleated shade face down, mark for rings down the center back of each pleat, starting at the top of the facing and to the top, spacing between 6 and 8 inches (15.2 and 20.3 cm). Sew rings at each mark, catching the face fabric. Do not catch the pleats underneath with the stitches.

10. Cut a metal or wooden dowel to fit between the rings. Cover with a sleeve of lining and sew to each bottom ring. This will keep the pleats spaced evenly. **(I)**

11. Cut a board to the finished size and mount the shade to the board. For this shade, additional welt cord was stapled along the top **(J)** and the matching fabric was stapled snug next to the welt cord with tack strip, then flipped over and wrapped around the board. **(K)** (See Chapter 7: Installing Window Treatments.)

12. Add screw eyes under the board above each column of rings. Tie cord to the bottom rings and thread through the rings with RingLocks or cord shroud and screw eyes and out one side, leaving extra cord for pulling up and adjusting the shade.

Fold the pleats on each side and measure to make sure they are evenly placed.

Press the pleats from the front and pin.

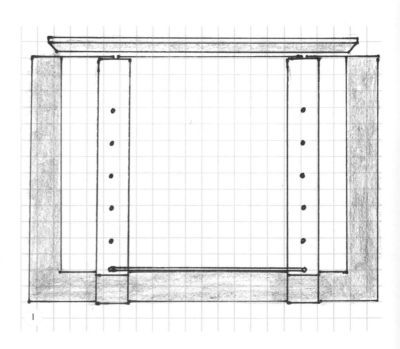

A view of the back before board mounting.

13. Install the shade on L-brackets. Pull the cords until the shade is to the desired height and tie off, or use a cord-adjusting orb to hold the shade in position. Tie a knot under the orb to prevent it from slipping and cut off excess cord, or add a cord cleat discretely behind the shade to wrap excess cord.

14. Dress the shade by lifting the tails on each side and smoothing the folds evenly to drop down. Even out the folds in the center to create a swag look. Tug down on the crease of each side of the pleats, folding neatly to allow the amount of fullness you want to show. The shade can be dressed to have a horn or an inverted pleat where it is pulled up with cord. Select whichever you like best! (L)

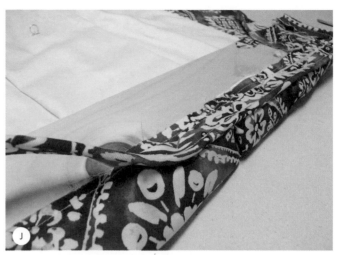

Welt cord is added at the front edge of the board to match what was sewn to the shade.

Wrap fabric around the board, finishing the top.

London shades need to be dressed to neaten the folds and to create a symmetrical design.

TOP TREATMENTS

Top treatments are purely decorative, adding color, pattern, and beautiful shapes to the tops of windows. Swags, cornice boards, and pleated and gathered valances all serve as top treatments. Pair with draperies or shades to create a stunning overall design.

Many techniques for curtains and shades are used when making top treatments, only they're scaled to fit above the window. Many top treatments are mounted to boards, but decorative hardware can be used as well. There are endless possibilities.

Valances

Valances should be mounted above the window, raised up above and covering the top of the frame and a few inches of the window glass. You want to avoid a top-heavy appearance. Scale drawings or paper patterns can be used to determine good proportions.

Since top treatments and valences are viewed from below, be conscious of the lining and edge finishes. It looks more attractive to have a matching or contrast color for the lining and trims such as welt cords, ruffles, or fringe along the bottom.

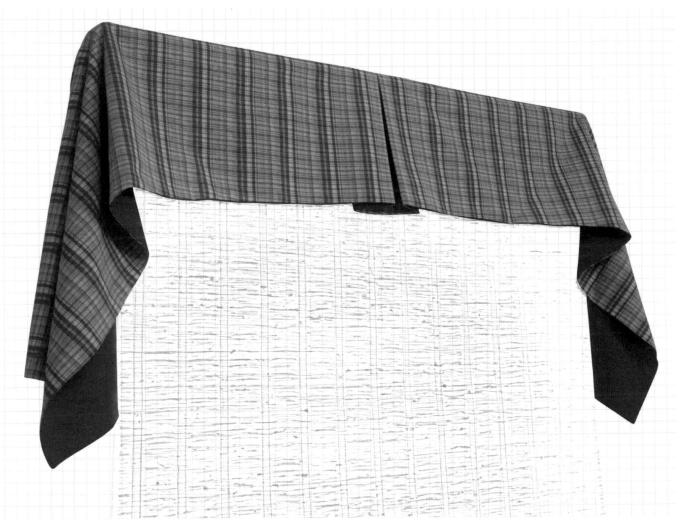

A shawl valance can be easily altered for a variety of different looks.
A pleat was added to the center of this valance.

SHAWL VALANCE

This style has a very simple design. The fabric falls over the shoulders, or ends of the mounting board, to create jabots on each end. It's a simple, versatile design that works on any window and is a breeze to install.

Three versions are shown on the same window to illustrate how easy it is to alter the pattern for different looks. The valances shown are installed with hook-and-loop tape. This makes installation so easy! If you would like a top treatment that can be removed for cleaning, the shawl valance would be an excellent choice.

Just about any fabric is suitable. If a very thin fabric is used, add interlining for body. A heavy fabric will not drape into pleats as well, so you may need to tack the folds by hand or with a tacking gun to control flaring.

Because the lining fabric will show, plan to use a complementary color. For more detail, a small welt cord, banding, or trim can be added to the edges.

Getting Started

Begin by making a sample with lining or muslin fabric to determine how much length and width would look best for your window.

What You Will Need

- decorator fabric
- lining fabric
- mounting board
- Velcro
- heavy-duty stapler and staples
- tools and hardware for installation

Yardage Requirements

To most accurately determine how much fabric you will need, cut the board and drape muslin to the finished width and length. The fabric will extend past the board on each end. The size of the board is added to the front drop. The valance will be a large rectangle. Add seam allowances to all sides.

Cut board length ____ + fabric allowance for a jabot on each end ____ = finished width

Finished width ____ ÷ fabric width ____ = number of cuts needed

Length or center drop of the finished valance ___ + board size ___ = cut length

Number of cuts ___ x cut length ___ ÷ 36 inches (91.4 cm) = total yards (meters)

Note: If using a solid or nondirectional print, the fabric can be railroaded.

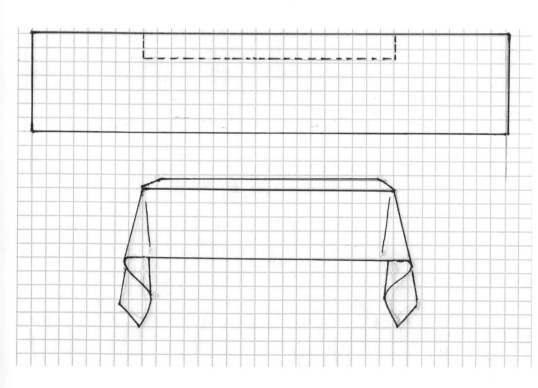

A rectangle of fabric is used to make a basic shawl valance. The fabric will extend past the board on each side.

A

Cut face fabric and lining to the same size.

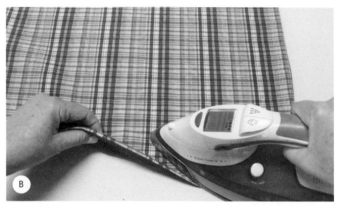

B

Press the front and back to create neat edges.

C

Pin and sew loop strip to the valance, centered across the back.

Making a Shawl Valance

1. Sew together the face fabric and lining and cut to the size needed, adding seam allowances. On this valance, the lining fabric was railroaded for no seams. (A)

2. Place the fabrics face-to-face, pin, and sew around all four sides, leaving an opening at the center top for turning.

3. Clip corners and turn right sides out. Press all the edges and close the opening by hand sewing or by ironing with fusible web tape. (B)

4. Cut a piece of sew-on loop strip the finished width of the mounting board. Pin to the top back of the valance, centered along the edge. Sew the loop strip to the valance. (C)

5. Staple hook strip along the back edge of the mounting board.

6. Install the mounting board to the wall using L-brackets. The hook strip should be next to the wall. Install the valance by centering the valance and pressing the hook-and-loop strip together. The extra fabric will fall down into folds at each side of the board.

7. Install the shawl valance to the mounting board and dress each end to look symmetrical. (See Chapter 7: Installing Window Treatments.) (D)

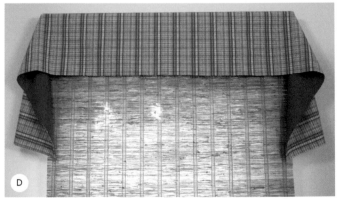

D

The shawl valance is board mounted. Extra length on each end forms a cascade or jabot effect.

PLEATED AND SHAPED SHAWL VALANCES

To create a pleated valance, add 12 inches (30.5 cm) extra to the finished width. After the valance is sewn, turned, and pressed, fold a pleat in the center of the rectangle. Sew on loop strip and it's ready to install.

The bottom edge can also be shaped. Plan this by determining the short and long point on your window. Pin a rectangle of muslin to the mounting board and cut away to the desired shape, or draw on the muslin with a marker. Mark half the window and then fold in half to cut the rest of the pattern.

Use the muslin pattern to cut face and lining fabrics, adding for seam allowances. Sew fabrics together, turn, and press. Attach loop strip and install.

Add dimension to the shawl valance with pleats.

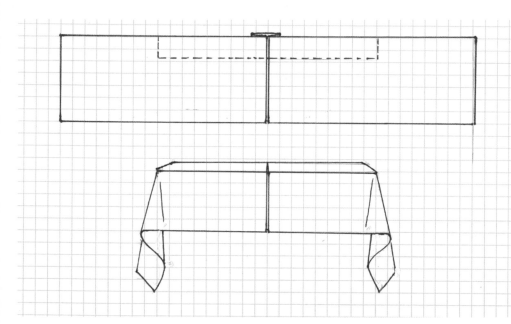

Allow an additional 12 inches (30.5 cm) in width for the center pleat.

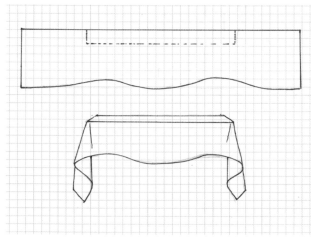

Add a shape to the bottom.

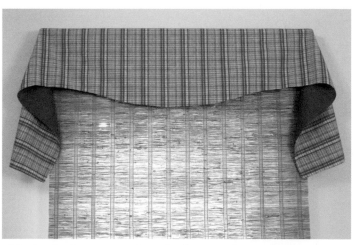

This shawl valance curves down in the center for a softer shape.

BOX PLEATED

Box-pleated valances can be very simple with straight lines, or more complex with shaped edges and contrast pleats, as is shown in this instruction. The flat sections across the valance are called "boxes" and are divided by flat, inverted pleats.

The basic box-pleated valance is simple to make. Use a wrapped hem to join the face fabric and lining. Pleats are typically 10 to 12 inches (25.4 to 30.5 cm) in size with a half pleat on each end, or a full pleat if the pleats are contrast lined.

You can be very creative with this style. The "boxes" can be uniform or of different sizes. The bottom can be shaped, and details like buttons, banding, trims, and contrast fabrics can be used to create a unique design. A scale drawing is a helpful tool when planning the size and shape of the repeating boxes. For shaped valances, a complementary color lining or facing is needed because the lining on the bottom edge is visible.

Getting Started

When planning your valance, there isn't a rule for the number of "boxes." The decision can be based on the proportions of the width and length, fabric motif, or overall feel or personal aesthetic. Anything goes! If using a patterned fabric, fold up the fabric before cutting to see how it will look with different widths of boxes and pleats.

Medium-weight cotton or cotton-blend home décor fabrics work best. Look for fabrics that are not too soft and stretchy and that can be ironed with heat and steam. Interlining, interfacing, or stabilizers can be used to add body to thin fabrics.

What You Will Need

- decorator fabric
- lining
- mounting board
- small-diameter welt cord
- heavy-duty stapler and staples
- tools and hardware for installation

This box-pleated valance features contrast-lined pleats and welt cord.

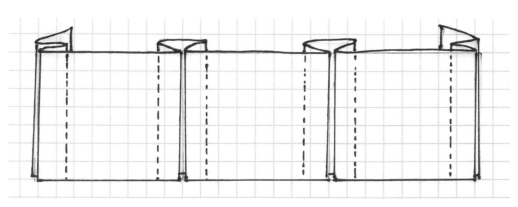

The pleats are folded to the reverse side.

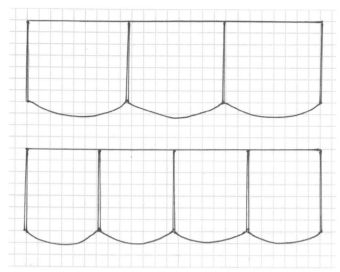

Two design ideas for the same window.

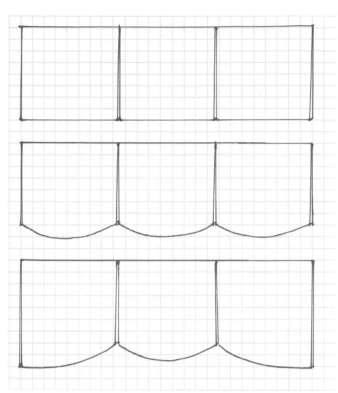

Three ideas for a box-pleated valance, straight and shaped.

Plan the box sizes by looking at the fabric motif. The larger size boxes create a mismatched design.

A smaller size box pleat will match perfectly!

Yardage Requirements

MAIN FABRIC

Measure your window and determine the finished width, long point, and short point. For solid or allover patterns, the fabric can be cut on the straight, or railroaded. Plan for two and a half times fullness. The lining can be railroaded even if the face fabric is not.

Finished width ___ + returns ___ x 2 fullness = ___ ÷ fabric width = ___ number of cuts needed

Number of cuts x finished length = ___ ÷ 36 inches (91.4 cm) = ___ yards (meters)

If using a fabric with a pattern repeat and prominent motif, a paper pattern should be made first and then this can be used to estimate yardage. You may need one pattern motif for each flat section, or if the fabric is printed with designs side-by-side, you may be able to get two flat sections within one repeat.

Making the Paper Pattern

1. Sketch the valance to scale on graph paper and enlarge to full size on pattern paper. Cut out the design. You can tape this on the window to check proportions. (A)

2. Each section is cut out and the pattern is enlarged with 12-inch (30.5 cm) pleat sections. (B)

3. Fold up the pattern and check the size and shape. (C)

4. Mark for seams inside the pleats so they will be hidden from the front. Use a different color marker so the seams will not be confused with folded edges. (D)

5. Cut the pattern apart at the lines drawn for the seams. The pattern pieces are ready to use for cutting the fabric. (E)

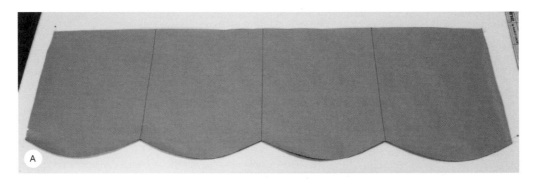

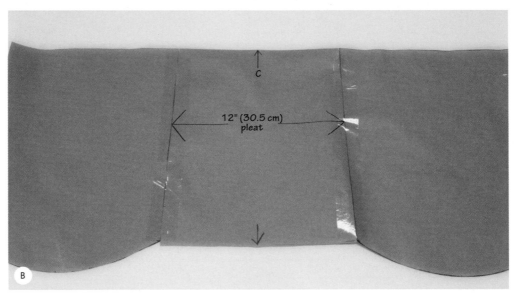

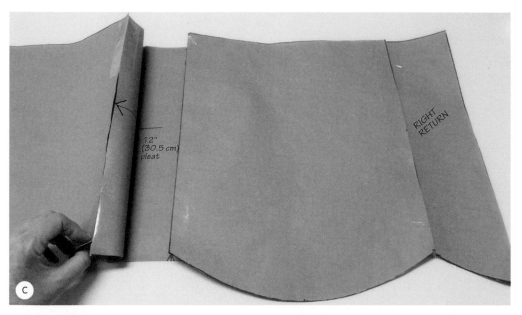

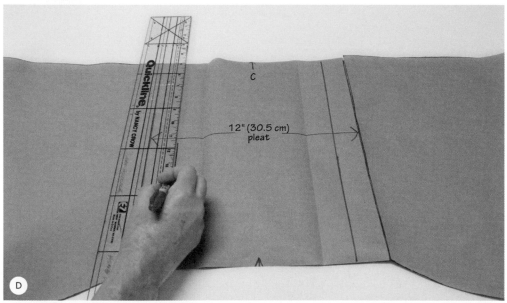

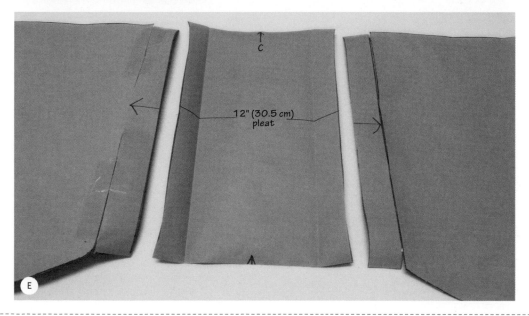

Add allowances when cutting around the pattern pieces.

All the pieces are cut and ready to sew together.

Sew the pieces together and press the seams open.

Sew welt cord to the bottom edge.

Making a Box-Pleated Valance

1. Place the pattern pieces on the fabric. Make sure the pattern is level and the fabric pattern motif is centered. Pin the pattern to the fabric and draw a ½-inch (1.3 cm) seam allowance around the edges. (See Chapter 7: Installing Window Treatments.) ***Note:*** For a valance waistband sewn to the top, add a ½-inch (1.3 cm) seam allowance. For a valance that is stapled to the board, add 2 inches (5 cm) to the top of the pattern. **(A)**

2. Cut out each section. A solid red fabric is used for the pleats. **(B)** Sew the pieces together in order and press the seams open. **(C)** Cover and sew small welt cord to the bottom edge, clipping around curves. **(D)** (See Chapter 3: Fundamental Techniques.)

3. Place the lining face up on the table with the valance on top, face down. Cut the lining to fit, pin together across the bottom, and sew next to the welt cord. **(E)** Sew a ½-inch (1.3 cm) seam up each return end. Do not sew across the top. Trim off seam allowances to ¼ inch (6 mm). **(F)** Turn right sides out and press on the front and back. **(G)**

4. Measure and mark the length and trim off excess even across the top. Pin and sew to hold the top together.

5. Mark the pleats using the pattern pieces as a guide and fold into place. **(H)** Use quilter's clips to hold the pleats together across the bottom, keeping the valance neat and flat. **(I)** Measure across the width and make any adjustments needed.

6. A waistband and Velcro finish the top. **(J)** Install the valance board to the wall using L-brackets and mount the valance on top. If needed, a tacking gun can be used to help keep the pleats from flaring open. **(K)** (See Chapter 7: Installing Window Treatments.)

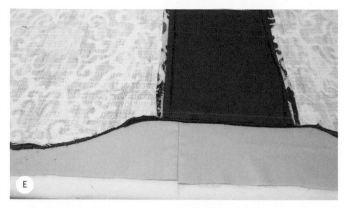

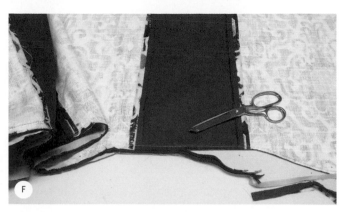

Place the valance face down on the lining.

Sew together and trim the seam allowances.

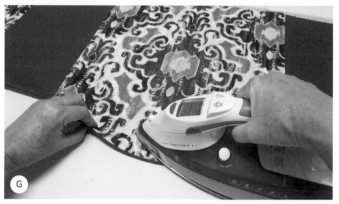

Press on the front and back, smoothing the fabric up toward the top.

Mark the pleats with pins and fold over the front sections, meeting in the center.

Use quilter's clips to keep the pleats together at the bottom.

This valance has a waistband with Velcro for easy installation.

A tacking gun is used to control flare. Hide the tacks inside the pleats.

SCALLOPED VALANCE WITH HORNS

A bold, damask print is highlighted with this valance design.

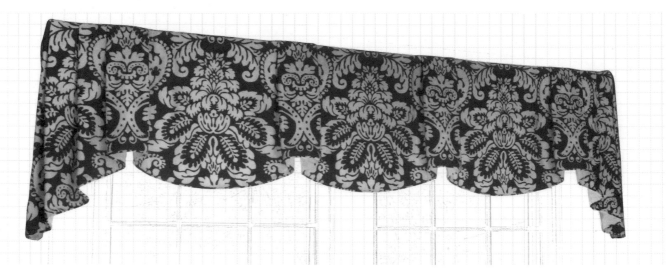

Getting Started

This valance style combines flat, shaped sections with horns and cascades, which can be pleated or gathered. The lining shows, so a matching color should be used or a facing applied to the reverse side. Interlining was used to add body and enhance the white background.

What You Will Need

- decorator fabric

- lining and interlining (interlining is optional)

- mounting board

- welt cord

- heavy-duty stapler and staples

- tools and hardware for installation

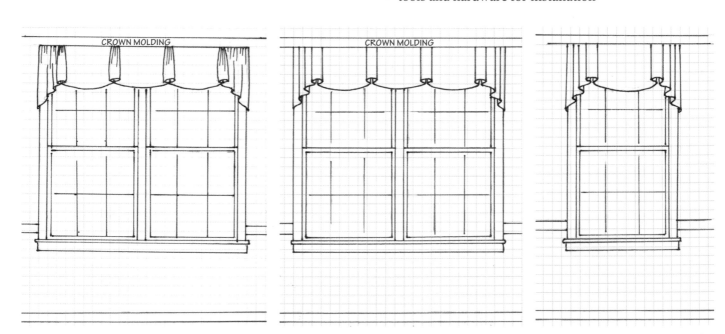

Gathered horns and cascades have a soft, feminine look.

Flat horns and cascades are more tailored.

For single windows, only one scalloped section is used.

Yardage Requirements

Measure your window and determine the finished width, long point, and short point. For solid or allover patterns, the fabric can be cut on the straight, or railroaded. Plan for two times fullness. Lining and interlining can also be railroaded even if the face fabric is not.

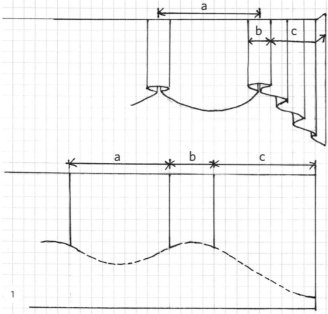

1

a. Measurement from the center of each horn
b. Measurement across the front of the horn, doubled
c. Measurement across cascade and return, doubled

MAIN FABRIC

Finished width ___ + returns ___ x 2 fullness = ___ ÷ fabric width = ___ number of cuts needed

Number of cuts x finished length = ___ ÷ 36 inches (91.4 cm) = ___ yards (meters)

If using a fabric with a pattern repeat and prominent motif, a paper pattern should be made first and then this can be used to estimate yardage. You may need one pattern motif for each flat section, or if the fabric is printed with designs side-by-side, you may be able to get two flat sections within one repeat. The horns will also need to match across the valance.

Making the Paper Pattern

1. Sketch a drawing to scale on graph paper. Enlarge the width on pattern paper following the second illustration.

2. Use the short and long points to sketch a curved line across the bottom. You don't need to draw the whole valance, only the three sections. (A)

3. After the pattern is drawn and cut out, you can fold up the paper to check the design. Now is the time to make adjustments to the shape. Once you are satisfied with the shape, cut out each individual piece. (B)

The individual pattern pieces are ready.

Making notes on the pattern will prevent mistakes when cutting.

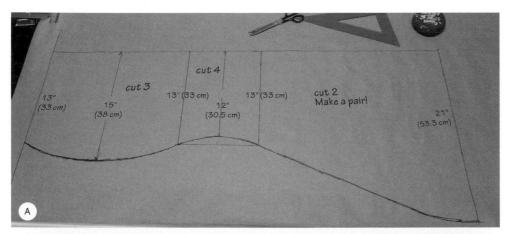

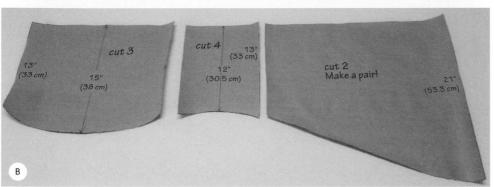

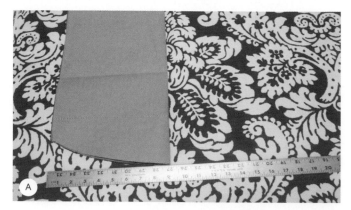

Fold the pattern piece in half to center the design.

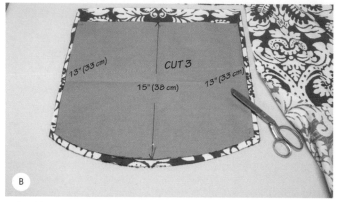

Add allowances to the pattern for seams and board mounting.

Press the seams open on the back.

Cut the interlining to match the face fabric.

Making a Scalloped Valance with Horns

1. Place the pattern pieces on the fabric. Make sure the pattern is level and the fabric pattern motif is centered. (A) Pin the pattern to the fabric and draw a ½-inch (1.3 cm) seam allowance around the edges. **Note:** For a valance waistband sewn to the top, add a ½-inch (1.3 cm) seam allowance. For a valance that is stapled to the board, add 2 inches (5 cm) to the top of the pattern. (B)

2. Cut out each piece and then use them to cut other matching pieces. For each cascade, you will need opposites—be sure to turn the pattern over so that the pieces make a pair.

3. Sew the sections together and press the seams open. (C)

4. Cut the lining and interlining. Place the seamed valance face up on the interlining and iron to make sure the pieces are flat and neat. Cut out the shape (D) and glue-baste the edge of the valance to the interlining using small dots of fabric glue. (E)

5. Cover welt cord and sew to the bottom edge of the interlined valance front. This can also be glue-basted first if the fabric is slippery or there is take-up with sewing. (F)

6. Place the lining face up and the interlined valance front with welt cord face down on top. Cut off excess lining, pin, and sew next to the welt cord. At each end, sew a ½-inch (1.3 cm) seam.

7. Trim the seam allowance to ¼ inch (6 mm). (G) Turn the valance right sides out and press on the front and back. (H) Pin together the top edge.

8. Fold and pin the pleats for each horn and the cascades into evenly spaced pleats, allowing the return to be flat. (I)

9. Measure across the width, checking the size. Some adjustments can be made by letting pleats out or taking them in to fit. The valance is ready for a waistband to be sewn to the top, or to be stapled to the board. (J)

10. Install the valance board to the wall using L-brackets. (See Chapter 7: Installing Window Treatments.) The cascades might require a little pressing, but don't overly press the horns. They should have some flare and not be flattened. (K)

Glue-baste to hold the face fabric to the interlining, eliminating the need for a lot of pins.

Apply welt cord to the bottom edge. This makes turning and pressing the curves easier, and it looks more professional. It's worth the extra step!

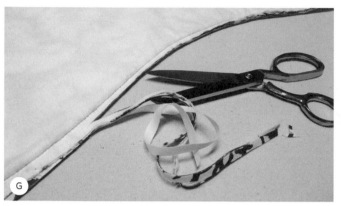

Trim the seam allowance rather than making clips around the curves that could show when light shines through the valance.

Press the valance all over before folding the pleats.

Fold pleats for the horns and then flatten and pin in place.

Measure to make sure the width is accurate. Don't be discouraged if the size isn't perfect; it can be easily adjusted.

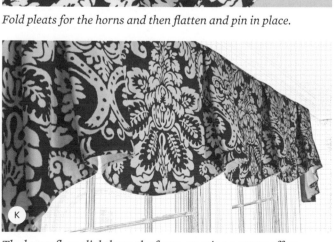

The horns flare slightly on the front, creating a pretty effect.

GATHERED VALANCE

Rod pocket valances are very popular and can be installed on decorative hardware or on plain white utility rods. For this valance, a white pole rod with finials was used, and you will see a clever solution for adding a return to the rod pocket, so that the valance looks neat and finished at the sides.

This pretty floral valance is gathered on a pole rod.

Getting Started

Select light- to medium-weight fabrics. Complementary fabric should be used for the lining because it will show at the short points. A small covered welt cord in the seam makes turning the edges easier and gives a polished look. Fringe or banding can also be used to embellish the bottom edge.

What You Will Need

- decorator fabric
- lining
- small-diameter welt cord
- tools and hardware for installation

Yardage Requirements

MAIN FABRIC AND LINING

Measure your window and determine the finished width, long point, and short point. For solid or allover patterns, the fabric can be cut on the straight, or railroaded. Plan for two and half times fullness. Lining fabric can be railroaded even if the face fabric is not.

For the rod pocket, measure around the pole or rod with a flexible tape measure. Do not make the rod pocket too tight; it should slide on and off the rod easily. For the ruffle above the rod pocket, allow 1 to 3 inches (2.5 to 7.6 cm). Add together the rod pocket and top ruffle and multiply times two. Use this for the calculations at right (rod pocket and top ruffle).

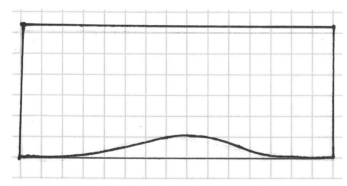

Draw a pattern for half the valance shape.

Finished width ___ + returns ___ x 2.5 fullness = ___ ÷ fabric width = ___ number of cuts needed

Finished length (longest point) ___ + rod pocket and top ruffle ___ + ½ inch (1.3 cm) seam allowance = cut length

Number of cuts x cut length = ___ ÷ 36 inches (91.4 cm) = ___ yards (meters)

If using a fabric with a pattern repeat, take this into consideration for the cut length.

Cut length = ___ ÷ pattern repeat = ___ (round up) = number of pattern repeats for each cut

Pattern repeat ___ x number of pattern repeats for each cut = _____ cut length adjusted for pattern matching

Making a Gathered Valance

1. Cut a piece of muslin or pattern paper the finished cut length of the valance x 1.25 the width. This will be half of the finished valance. Mark the short point and long points and draw a curved line between the marks.

2. Cut the fabrics and seam together. Press the seams open.

3. Fold over a doubled hem or heading across the top of the seamed face fabric for the rod pocket and ruffle heading. For example, if your rod pocket is 2 inches (5 cm) and the ruffle is 1 inch (2.5 cm), you will make a 3-inch (7.6 cm) heading, requiring 6 inches (15.2 cm) of fabric.

4. Press the doubled heading and then fold the valance in half, face together, neat and square.

5. Use the pattern to draw the curved shape across the bottom, adding a ½-inch (1.3 cm) seam allowance, and cut the curved shape. (A)

Cut the curved shape across the bottom of the valance fabric.

Pin the front piece with welt cord attached to the lining.

Cut off excess fabric below the welt cord.

Press the edges and the entire valance front and back.

6. Cover enough small-diameter welt cord to go across the bottom edge. Sew to the bottom edge, following the curved shape. (See Chapter 3: Fundamental Techniques.)

7. Place the face fabric with welt cord attached face down on the lining that is face up. Smooth, straighten, and press. Pin together the bottom edge for sewing. (B)

8. Sew across the bottom edge, stitching close to the welt cord. Sew each end using a ½-inch (1.3 cm) seam allowance. Leave the top open.

9. Cut away excess fabric below the welt cord. Cut close to the cord, leaving a ¼-inch (6 mm) seam allowance. (C)

10. Turn the valance right sides out. Press from the front and back. (D)

11. With the valance face down, fold over the top rod pocket and ruffle heading. Press and pin for sewing. Draw a line to follow for the ruffle along the back of the heading. Sew two rows of stitching: the bottom edge of the doubled heading and along the line drawn for the top ruffle. (E)

12. Use a compensating foot or walking foot on the machine to keep the layers of fabric from bunching up as you sew. If you don't have specialty feet for your machine, make small tucks in the fabric as you sew. The tucks will be on the back and they will not show when the valance is gathered.

13. For valances on pole rods with finials and brackets, a return is needed. To do this, measure and mark the size of the return on the rod pocket, on the front of the valance. (F)

14. Carefully cut a slit in the face fabric and one layer of lining below. *Do not cut all* the way through. (G)

15. Tuck under the cut edges and use fabric glue to finish like a buttonhole. Just use a little glue to finish the edges. You don't want to glue together the rod pocket! (H)

16. Slide the rod from the font into one of the holes cut in the rod pocket and out the other, gathering the valance on the rod. (I)

17. Install on the window with brackets. Dress the valance so it is evenly gathered. (See Chapter 7: Installing Window Treatments.)

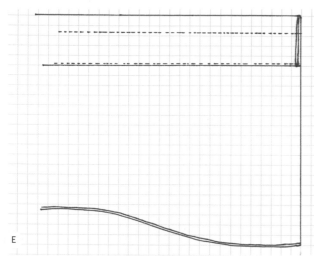

Sew two horizontal rows of stitching, one at the bottom edge of the pocket and one above to create the bottom of the ruffle.

Mark the distance for the return from the rod to the wall.

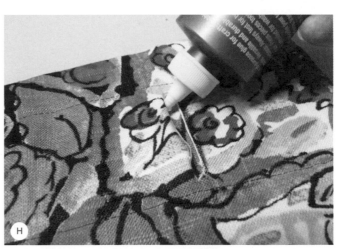

Cut a slit through the face fabric and one layer of lining and tuck under the edges.

Add a little fabric glue to hold the cut folded edges together like a buttonhole.

Slide the rod into the pocket.

Black welt cord outlines the bottom shape.

Swags

Swags are a classic and traditional window treatment, gracing windows in formal rooms for centuries. The shape of this style incorporates pleats and draped curves, combining structure and softness in one design.

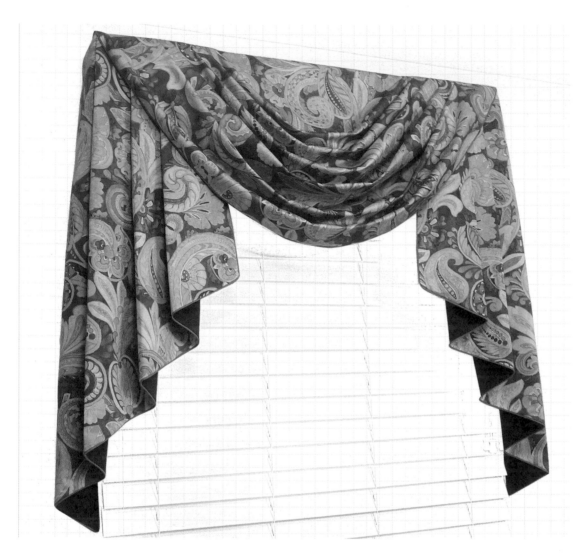

Classic pleated swag and jabots.

TRADITIONAL SWAG AND JABOTS

One swag can be used, but the wider the window, the deeper the swag will need to be, so it's best to use more than one swag on windows over 40 inches (102 cm) wide. Multiple swags can be overlapped left to right, or if using an odd number the center swag can be on top. Swags can also be butted together end-to-end with a short jabot placed in between to cover the short point.

You can use swags without jabots, hanging them over draperies or cornice boards, or wrapping the pleats around a boxed corner.

Getting Started

Select medium-weight decorator fabrics that will drape softly. Some fabrics like silk will benefit from interlining. On this style the lining will show on the jabots, so a complementary color or pattern is recommended.

Plan to mount the board above the window, high enough for the swags to cover the frame or window opening and 1 inch (2.5 cm) beyond on each side. When installing swags and jabots over curtains or draperies, allow 1½ to 2 inches (3.8 to 5 cm) extra per side to clear the fullness of the fabric.

Plan to add a small-diameter welt cord in the seams. This may seem like extra work, but it will make turning and pressing the bias edges much easier, and it adds a beautiful, professional finish!

What You Will Need

- muslin for pattern drafting
- decorator fabric
- lining
- small-diameter welt cord
- mounting board
- heavy-duty stapler and staples
- tools and hardware for installation

Yardage Requirements and Pattern Drafting

Draft the swag and jabot patterns on lining or muslin fabric and use this to figure accurately how much yardage you will need. Generally, swags require at least 48 inches (122 cm) of fabric, and each jabot will need the finished length plus a few extra inches for seams and board mounting. Swags are often cut on the bias, but cutting them on the straight of grain, or even railroaded, works fine, too. A bias cut does drape easier, but with fabrics that have a vertical print or design like stripes, toiles, or botanical designs, cutting on the bias will make your finished swags look tilted and awkward. The jabots are best cut on the straight of grain.

For large swags you may need to seam fabrics together. Plan for the seams to be at the sides, and not in the middle of the swag.

Drape a cord at the window in the shape of a swag to the desired length, securing it to the wall with pushpins or blue painter's tape. Measure the length or drop for the center point of the swag. Mark the cord, straighten, and measure. This is the width of the bottom hem of the swag.

Measure the short point and long point for the jabots. A general guideline is to have the short point of the jabot be similar to the center drop of the swag. This can be adjusted to alter the finished look.

Making the Swag Pattern

The first time you drape a swag it might feel challenging. The more you practice, the easier it will be. As you drape the pattern, step back and look at it from a distance. Take your time; drafting the pattern is the time well spent!

Use multiple swags on wide windows, overlapping the pleats.

A center jabot covers the short point on swags that are butted together.

Swags used without jabots, hanging over pleated draperies.

1. To make the swag pattern, cut a piece of muslin on the straight of grain, or on the bias.

Width = measurement of the draped cord + 4 inches (10.2 cm)

Length = center drop of the swag x 2.5

For example, if the draped cord measured 50 inches (127 cm) and the center drop is 18 inches (45.7 cm), you will cut a piece of muslin 54 inches (137.2 cm) wide by 45 inches (114.3 cm) long.

2. Draw a line on the pattern down the center, from the top to the bottom, and another horizontally 2 inches (5 cm) from the top. From the center, mark one-third of the finished width. This will give you general spacing for the open area in the center. For example, if the finished width of the swag is 40 inches (102 cm), one-third of the width is 13.3 inches (33.8 cm) (round up to 14 inches [35.5 cm]). At the center top, mark 7 inches (17.8 cm) on each side of the centerline.

3. Mark a pinnable surface (sewing table or ironing board) with tape, marking the finished swag width and center point.

4. Starting in the center, pin the muslin across the center section. Using your hands, pinch together a pleat using approximately 4 or 5 inches (10.2 or 12.7 cm) of fabric and lift up, pinning in place at the mark. Repeat for the opposite side. (A)

5. Continue lifting and pinning pleats, trying to keep them evenly spaced 1 to 2 inches (2.5 to 5 cm) apart. You will pull up five pleats on each side.

6. As you form pleats, pin them in place across the top. Stand back and review the swag. Unpin and adjust as needed to get an even look. Measure to see if the swag is the correct length in the center. You may need to adjust the folds by letting them out to achieve a longer length, or taking them up to make the swag shorter. (B)

7. After the swag is evenly folded, step back and look over the swag. You will use one half of the swag to continue with the pattern, so choose whether the right or left looks best. This will be the side you use to draft the rest of the pattern.

8. Cut off the extra fabric at the top of the pleats, evenly across. (C)

9. At the bottom of the swag, cut away excess fabric to create a rounded shape on the preferred half of the pattern. (D)

10. After the top and bottom are shaped, unpin the pattern, lay it flat, and fold in half along the centerline.

11. Cut the opposite side to match. The sides will be in a zigzag shape. (E)

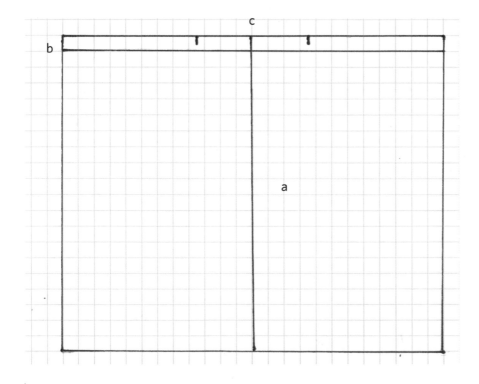

Mark the muslin:
a. Center from top to bottom
b. Horizontal line 2 inches (5 cm) from the top edge
c. One-third of the finished swag width

Lift the fabric up and pin, making pleats across the top and rounded folds on the front.

Measure the center point on the swag pattern.

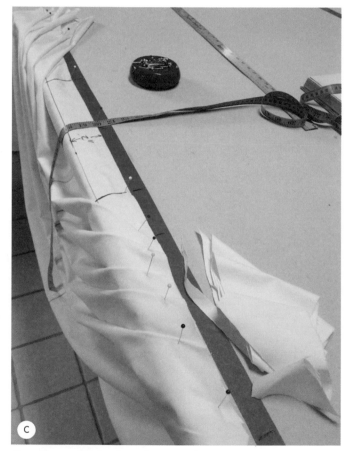

Cut off extra fabric above the swag pleats.

Cut away excess fabric to make a rounded shape at the bottom.

Fold in half and cut the other half of the swag pattern to match.

12. At the top, cut away the angular shape on each side straight up, at a right angle. **(F)**

13. Check the swag pattern by folding it up again, and pinning in place. Make any adjustments needed. **(G)**

14. The swag pattern is finished and ready to use for cutting the main fabrics.

Cut off the top angled pieces.

F

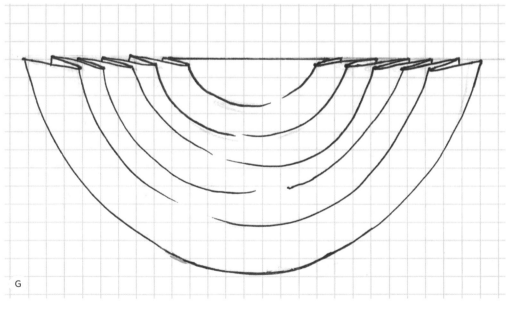

Fold the angled cuts into pleats across the top.

G

Making the Jabot Pattern

1. To make the jabot pattern, follow the illustration, starting with 4 inches (10.2 cm) on the leading edge, 8-inch (20.3 cm) pleats, 2-inch (5 cm) spaces, and the return. For the jabots shown, the front edge is slightly angled. You can do this if you like the look, or make the front edge straight. **(A)**

2. Cut the shape from muslin and fold up, following the illustration. Fold in the pleats and check to see whether any adjustments need to be made. Make a note on the pattern to cut opposites, to make a matching pair. **(B)**

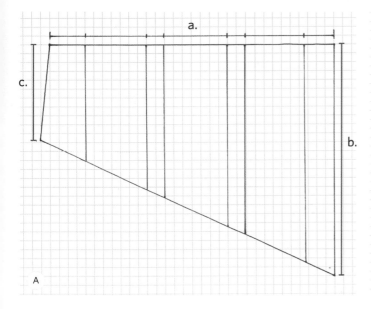

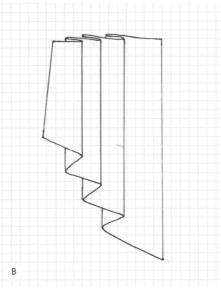

Jabot pattern:
a. 32 inches (81.3 cm) plus return based on your board size
b. Finished length
c. Short point

Fold the jabot pattern to check the shape and size.

Cutting the Fabric

1. Use the patterns to cut the main fabric pieces. With the fabric face up, lay the swag pattern over the fabric. Cut the bottom curve and to the outside of the angled cuts along the side. You do not need to cut to the angled shape. If using a fabric with a pattern motif, pay attention to where the motif will look best on the front of the swag, keeping in mind that the top center of the swag has the best space for showing off the pattern. You may want to raise the motif up, instead of centering it within the swag.

2. After the swag is cut, place it face down on the lining fabric and cut to match.

3. For the jabots, cut one using the pattern with the fabric face up, then use this piece face down on the fabric to cut the opposite jabot. If using a patterned fabric, make sure both jabots are cut at the same repeat, so that the pattern lines up evenly across the window from one side to the other. Add an extra inch or two (2.5 or 5 cm) at the top of the pattern for take-up. Place each jabot cut face down on the lining fabric and cut to match.

4. Cut bias strips and cover enough small welt cord to go around the swag, down the front edges, and across the bottom of the jabots. (See Chapter 3: Fundamental Techniques.)

Making the Traditional Swag

1. Sew covered welt cord to the bottom of the face swag piece. Pin the face and lining pieces together and sew next to the welt cord.

2. Trim away seam allowances to ¼ inch (6 mm) and turn right sides out.

3. Press the front and back.

4. Use the swag pattern to cut the shape. (A) (B)

5. Secure each angled cut with small pieces of iron-on fusible web. (C)

6. At the top, fold under the fabric on each side and join together with fusible web. (D)

7. Drape the swag and fold the pleats. (E)

8. Pin the pleats well to hold them in place. Sew a band across the top for attaching to the board. Because the swag will be over the jabots, a wider banding is used. This will stagger the bulk of the two overlapping pieces. (See Chapter 7: Installing Window Treatments.) (F)

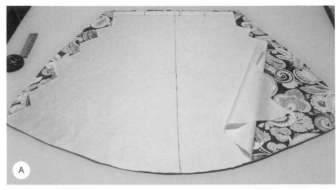

Place the swag pattern on top of the pressed and lined swag.

Cut out the shape, following the angles of the pattern.

Lift the edges and secure with fusible web.

Use fusible web to finish the top edges on the left and right sides.

Drape the finished swag.

Sew a band across the top of the swag.

Making the Jabots

1. Sew covered welt cord to the face pieces, down the front and across the bottom of each jabot. (A)

2. Pin together the face and lining pieces and sew together next to the welt cord and the return edge. Leave the top open for turning.

3. Trim away seam allowances next to the welt cord to ¼ inch (6 mm) and turn right sides out.

4. Press the front and back.

5. Measure the finished length, adding a seam allowance at the top, and cut off any excess. Sew or pin across the top. (B)

6. Fold up each jabot (C) and sew on a banding strip for installation. (D)

7. Cut board and cover with matching fabric. Staple the jabots to each end of the board and top with the swag, stapling it to the board.

8. Install the board above the window using L-brackets. Dress the swag folds by smoothing with your hands and adjusting the pleats.

Sew welt cord to the face jabot piece.

Measure and cut off excess fabric at the top.

Sew bands across the top of each jabot, mitering the corners.

Fold pleats in each jabot.

Small welt cord in a contrast color creates a decorative edge.

Silk fabric, flannel interlining, and fringe complement this style of swag and jabots.

ELEGANT GATHERED DOUBLE SWAG

Often a simpler construction method can be used to achieve the same results. That is the case with this style, which is gathered and easier to draft and sew than pleated versions. It is suitable for wide windows; add additional swag sections as needed.

Getting Started

Select light- to medium-weight decorator fabrics for the face and reverse sides. Silk was used for this window treatment, with flannel interlining for body and added insulation.

The reverse side of the jabots is visible, so plan for a fabric to be used in a matching or contrast color. The swags can be lined with standard drapery lining. Small welt cord is added to the seams, and it makes turning and pressing curved and angled edges easier.

The swags should measure 18 to 27 inches (45.7 to 68.6 cm) across. A jabot (or cascade) is used on each end and in the center. Plan to mount the valance above the window high enough for the swags to cover the frame or window opening. The valance board has vertical supports or "legs" on each side, which will need to clear the frame, so take that into account when planning the finished width.

This instruction is for the swags and jabots only; the draperies are optional. (To learn how to make the draperies, see Chapter 4: Curtains and Draperies.)

What You Will Need

- muslin or extra lining for pattern drafting
- decorator fabric
- lining and interlining (optional)
- pencil pleat shirring tape (with loop pile backing for attaching to Velcro hook strip)
- small-diameter welt cord
- boards cut to size for mounting the valance
- Velcro
- tools and hardware for installation

Yardage Requirements

The swags will use two and a half times the finished length. Plan for one cut per swag, which may require additional yardage if there is a pattern motif to match. Jabots will need two and a half times the finished width by the finished length, plus extra for board mounting. To figure exactly what you will need, make the muslin pattern first, and lay out the pieces. An equal amount of lining will be used.

Making the Swag Pattern

1. Mark half of the window size on a pinning board with low-tack tape. Drape a cord for the short and long points, reflecting the measurements taken at the window. This is the bottom shape of the swag. Pull the cord out straight and measure. This is the finished width at the bottom of the swag.

2. Cut a piece of muslin or lining for the swag pattern following the illustration. This is for one swag, or half the window. Pin the swag pattern across the top and gather up the edges, pinning in place until each side fits. (B) You can also run a long gathering stitch on each side and pull up each side. Neaten the folds and admire your swag! (C) If the measurement is too long or too short, adjust the gathers to achieve the perfect finished length.

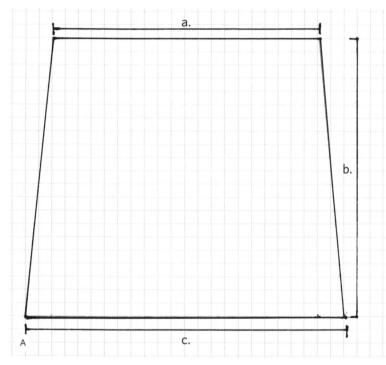

The swag pattern:
a. Finished width
b. Finished length x 2½
c. Measurement of draped cord

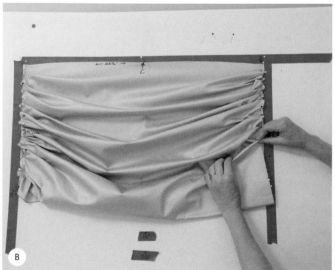

The fabric is pinned at the top and the sides are gathered to fit.

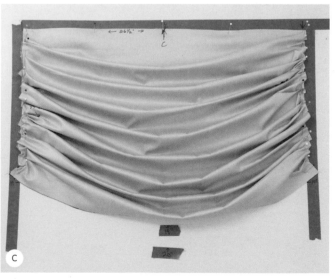

A swag pattern is drafted for half the window.

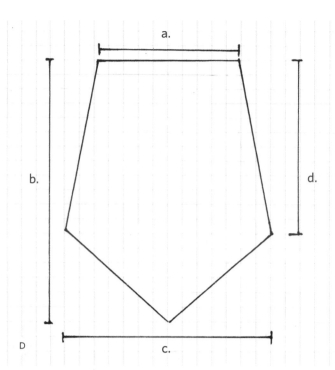

Center jabot:
a. 18 inches (45.7 cm)
b. Finished length
c. 22 inches (55.9 cm)
d. Short point

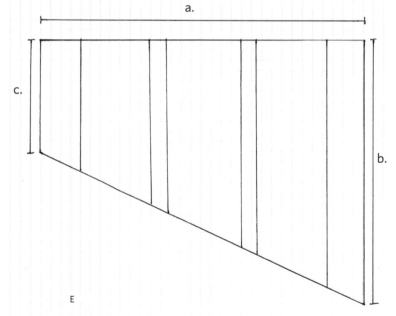

End jabots (make a pair):
a. 32 inches (81.3 cm) plus return based on your board size
b. Finished length
c. Short point

3. Draft a pattern for the center (D) and side (E) jabots using the short and long points based on your window measurements, following the illustrations at left. Use this as a guideline and add width or length as needed to achieve the desired shape.

4. Fold pleats in the jabot patterns. To pleat the center jabot, mark the center top and measure 6 inches (15.2 cm) on each side of the mark. Fold so that there are equal pleats, meeting in the center. Mark the side jabots as shown in the illustration, starting with 4 inches (10.2 cm) on the leading edge, 8-inch (20.3 cm) pleat, 2-inch (5 cm) space, 8-inch (20.3 cm) pleat, 2-inch (5 cm) space, 8-inch (20.3 cm) pleat, and the return. (F) Pin the pleats at the top and hang over the swag pattern to make sure the size and shape is satisfactory. (G) It is easy to make changes now, before cutting the main fabric.

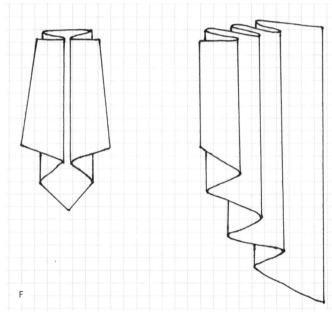

Fold pleats in the jabots.

Check the shape and size of the jabots with the swag pattern.

Making the Gathered Double Swag

1. Now that the swag and jabot patterns are finished it's time to cut the fabric, lining, and interlining! If using a fabric with a pattern motif, be sure to match all pieces.

2. With the fabric right side up, pin the swag pattern, center jabot, and one end jabot to the fabric and cut, allowing a ½-inch (1.3 cm) seam allowance around all sides. Cut an additional swag to match. Cut one more end jabot by turning over the one that was cut face down on the fabric, and cutting around the shape to make a pair.

3. Place all pieces face up on the interlining. Press over all the pieces and cut the interlining to match. The edges can be sewn or glue-basted to hold the fabric and interlining together. (A)

4. Cut linings to match. These swags will have white drapery lining. The jabots are lined in the same silk fabric.

5. Finish the swags by sewing together the two interlined pieces face-to-face, joining them in the middle. Press the seam open. Sew the lining cuts the same. Apply small welt cord to the bottom edge. Place the interlined swags and lining face-to-face and pin. Sew together across the bottom, getting close to the welt cord. Turn right sides out and press on the front and back. (B)

6. At each side, turn under the edges ½ inch (1.3 cm) and press. (C) Pin together and sew shirring tape on the back at each edge and down the center. Use a thread that matches the face fabric and sew over the bottom of the tape to secure the cords. (D) Leave cords loose at the top for pulling to gather the tape. Shirring tape with loop backing is used to attach to Velcro. **Note:** If using shirring tape without loop backing, you will sew Velcro loop strip to the edges after the swag is gathered.

A

The swag and jabot pieces are placed on top of the interlining, ready to be cut.

B

Sew swags together to make one large piece.

C

Press the edges on each side of the swags so the cut edges are turned inside.

D

Pin shirring tape to the center and side edges on the back of the swags and machine sew with a matching thread.

E

Pull the cords to gather the center and edges of the swags.

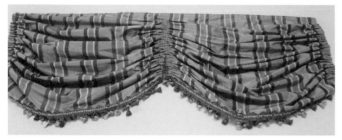

The gathered swags are finished.

F

The center jabot is ready to be sewn.

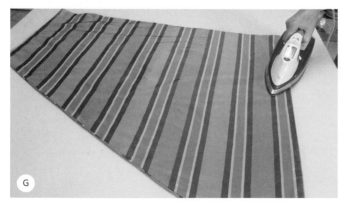

G

Press the jabots on the front and back.

7. Attach fringe to the bottom edge and a waistband along the top with Velcro for board mounting. Pull the cords, gathering the shirring tape to the correct length. Tie the cords securely and neaten the gathers. (To apply fringe, see Chapter 3: Fundamental Techniques; to attach a waistband, see Chapter 7: Installing Window Treatments.) (E)

8. Complete the jabots by sewing welt cord to the edges, pinning to the lining fabric and sewing next to the welt cord. (F) Trim seam allowances, turn right sides out, and press. (G)

9. Check the length measurement, trimming off excess fabric as needed. Apply fringe to the edges. On jabots, the fringe is applied on the front edges and down the bias edge. (H)

10. Pleat the jabots and add waistbands and Velcro for installation. (I) Because the jabots are mounted over the swags, the waistbands are made larger than what was sewn to the swag waistband, so that they are staggered and not mounted on top of each other. (J)

11. Cut board and cover with lining fabric. Attach end "leg" pieces with nails or screws, adding an L-bracket on the underside for stability. Staple hook strip Velcro to the top for the jabots and to the top and front edges of the legs for the swags. (K)

12. Install the board above the window using L-brackets. On this window treatment, decorative drapery panels are installed under the valance. Screw eyes were added under the mount board for drapery pins. (L) Attach the swag to the Velcro and top with the jabots. (M)

Apply fringe to the edges.

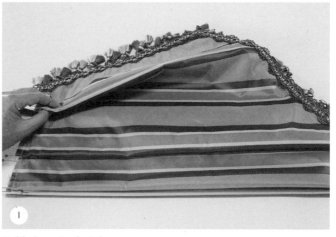

Fold pleats in the jabots.

The swags and jabots are finished and ready to install.

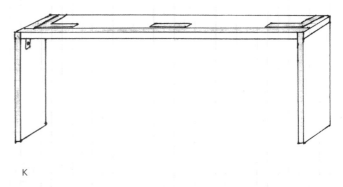

The valance board has legs on each end. Staple Velcro hook to the top and down the legs for attaching the swags and jabots.

Draperies are installed with screw eyes that have been added under the mount board.

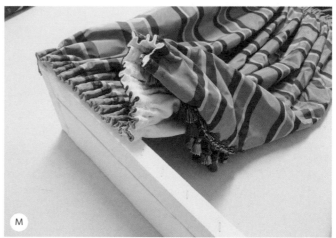

Attach the valance to the board. Check the fit.

CASUAL SWAG VALANCE WITH PLEATS

This style combines pleats with a relaxed or slouched center point to create a deep, scooped top. Decorative hardware adds to the design, making this a great companion style for open floor plans where other window treatments are used. Imagine this swag valance over a kitchen sink, using the same hardware as the draperies in the living room area.

Each swag section (between the pleats) should measure 16 to 21 inches (40.6 to 53.3 cm) wide and equal in length. Additional swag sections can be added to fit wider windows.

A less formal version of a swag, draped from a pole rod with rings.

Getting Started

Select light- to medium-weight decorator fabrics for the face and reverse sides. On this style the lining will show, so a complementary color or pattern is recommended.

Plan to mount the rod above the window high enough for the swags to cover the frame or window opening and 1 inch (2.5 cm) beyond on each side. This does require quite a bit of wall space above the window. If your window does not have enough space above for the swag to scoop, there is another option; mount to a flat cornice or pelmet with knobs or medallions to hide the window frame. (See illustration on page 180.)

What You Will Need

- muslin for pattern drafting
- decorator fabric
- lining
- decorative pole rod with brackets, finials, and rings
- tools and hardware for installation

Yardage Requirements

Drape a cord at the window, securing it to the wall with blue painter's tape to see how deep you would like the top scoop to be. Don't forget to allow room for the hardware, or you can mount the hardware first and then drape the cord. Mark the top points on the cord. The distance between the marks is the width needed across the top of the swags.

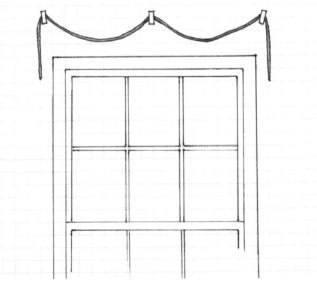

Tape a cord above the window to determine the center scoop on each swag section.

To figure how much fabric you will need, add 4 inches (10.2 cm) to the finished width and 4 inches (10.2 cm) to the finished length of each swag section. You should be able to cut two swags side-by-side. Add an additional 18 inches (45.7 cm) for the pleats. An average valance with two swags and three pleats will require 1½ yards (137 cm) of fabric for the face and for the lining. If using a fabric with a pattern motif, you may need additional fabric to cut matching pieces. To figure exactly what you will need, make the muslin pattern first and lay out the pieces. An equal amount of lining will be used.

Making the Pattern

1. For this project the window size is marked on a pinning board in the workroom, which is a fabulous place for draping patterns! You can also drape a pattern on a table or ironing board. A cord was draped for the top and bottom edges, reflecting the measurements taken at the window. This will provide a guide for drafting the pattern.

2. To drape a pattern, use scrap fabric or muslin. For this project the blue lining fabric was used. Cut a piece of fabric several inches larger than the finished width and length of the swag.

3. Start with the top scoop using the measurement made when draping the cord at the window, and pin that at the top corner. The fabric will relax between the pins and you will see a swag shape being created. (A)

4. Lift the fabric along the side edges and fold small pleats near the top corner. Pin in place to hold and copy the pleats on the other side. Two or three pleats can be used, depending on how deep and full you want the swag sections to be. This is the time to experiment! (B)

5. After the swag is shaped, draw the finished width and length on the fabric with a marker and cut off the excess fabric along the marked lines. (C)

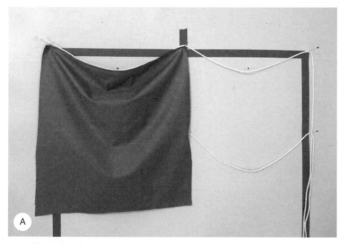

The fabric is draped to create the top scoop of one swag section.

Fold small pleats near the top corner on each side. This, combined with the relaxed, draped fabric, creates a very pretty swag shape.

Mark the finished size and shape and cut away the extra fabric.

Cutting the Fabric

1. Measure the short point on the swag and cut a piece of fabric this length by 8 inches (20.3 cm) for the pleat. Fold lengthwise into a tube and pinch together at the top and check it with the swag pattern to see how it looks. The bottom of the pleat should be even with the short point on the swag.

2. Unpin the swag pattern and lay it flat. Fold in half, matching up the two edges. One side might be slightly different than the other. Trim away the fabric so both sides match. If there is a huge difference in the angled shape, you may want to re-pin the pattern and adjust, or draft a new pattern.

3. The first and last pleats require extra fabric for the return. How much additional depends on the projection of the hardware. Add this to the left side of the left pleat, and the right side of the right pleat. Instead of a straight bottom edge, the return can be angled down slightly to the outside edge.

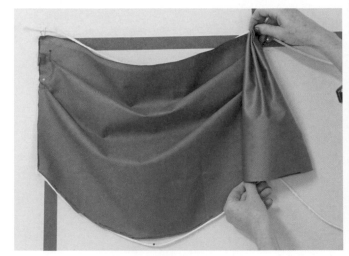

Make a pattern for the pleat and check to make sure it fits the swag.

Making a Casual Swag Valance with Pleats

1. Place the face fabric on the table face up. For print fabrics like this, determine which pattern motif will be used. Place the pattern pieces on the fabric, centering the motif. For the end pleats, be sure to place the pattern motif in the pleat area and not centered on the whole piece.

2. Mark a ½-inch (1.3 cm) seam allowance around all sides of the pattern pieces. As you cut one piece, you can use this as a template for the other cuts. You will cut out the number of pieces needed; for example, two swags, one center pleat, and two end pleats are used for this window. (A)

3. Place the lining fabric on the table face up, and then place the face fabric pieces face down on top. Pin to hold in place and cut to match.

4. Sew together the face and lining pieces along the top and bottom edges only. Turn the swags right sides out and press the seams.

5. Fold the small pleats along the sides of the swag pieces and pin to hold in place. You can check the shape and size of the finished swag by pinning it to the wall and making any adjustments needed. (B)

6. Starting with the center, place one of the swags inside the center pleat piece, lining up the edges. Pin together and sew. (C) Turn right sides out and press. Pin the next swag to the center pleat piece, only pinning the face pieces together. Sew and turn right sides out. The back will be open. Press under the edge, pin, and close the opening by hand stitching. (D)

7. Continue by adding the end pleat pieces in the same way, placing the swag inside the end pleat piece, pinning, and sewing together. (E) The openings along the end can be closed by hand sewing or by using a hem tape, as shown. (F)

The swag pattern is pinned to the main fabric and the seam allowance is marked.

Fold the angled cuts along the edge of the swag pieces to create small pleats.

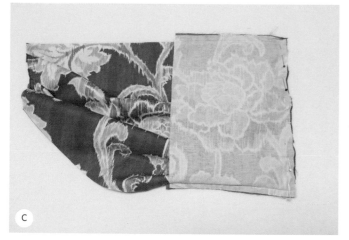

One of the swags is placed inside the center pleat section, sandwiched together and pinned, ready to sew.

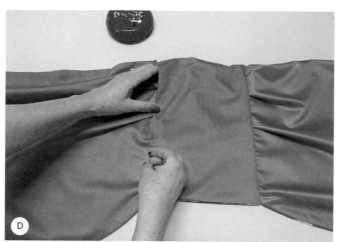

Both swags are sewn to the center pleat section. The back seam will need to be finished by hand sewing.

One of the end pleat sections is pinned to the swag and ready to sew.

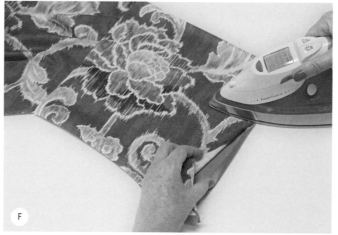

Fusible hem tape is a quick and easy way to finish the seams along the return edges.

8. Form pleats by folding the sections together. Each pleat will use about 7 inches (17.8 cm) of fabric. **(G)** Pin and sew with a matching thread from the top down 4 inches (10.2 cm). **(H)**

9. After the pleats are sewn, pinch together the top and hand stitch to create a Euro pleat and insert a drapery pin into the back. (See Chapter 4: Curtains and Draperies.) Check the valance by pinning it up to make sure it hangs properly.

10. Install the hardware. Attach the swag valance by inserting drapery pins into the eyelets on the rings and securing the returns to the wall. (See Chapter 7: Installing Window Treatments.)

A pleat is folded, pinned, and ready to sew.

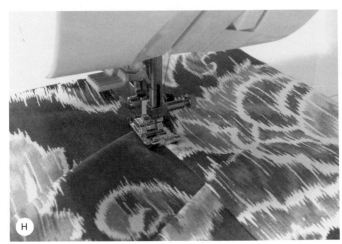

Sew the pleat using a matching thread and along the seam where the swag and pleat sections were joined.

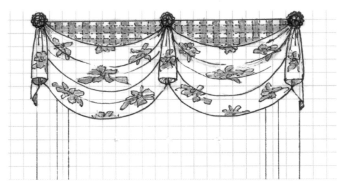

Mounting the swag valance to a cornice or pelmet lets you incorporate another fabric into the design, and covers the window frame.

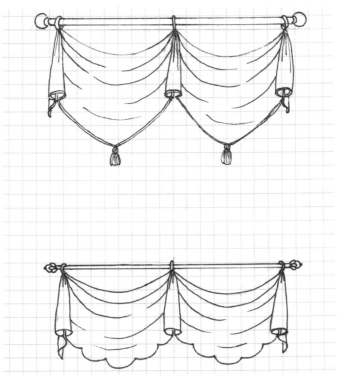

Design inspiration! For a variation of this style, change the bottom shape from rounded to pointed with a tassel or repeating scallops.

Cornice or Pelmet

Cornice or pelmet boards are a very structured and tailored window treatment. Fabric is applied to a wooden frame, or a heavyweight interfacing with batting to create an upholstered style. The bottom can be straight or cut into shapes.

UPHOLSTERED CORNICE BOARD

Cornice boards are a classic, timeless design suitable for any room. Shapes range from simple and straight, to curved and scalloped.

Getting Started

This style of top treatment is made with a wooden structure that is upholstered with batting and fabric. The example shown here is made with a base of low-loft batting that is somewhat flat. For a more rounded, soft look use a fluffier batting. One drawback of a highly padded surface is that it can show dimples and pulls in the fabric more easily so pre-lining by stretching and stapling a cover of interlining or muslin is suggested. This will create a firm base and you will not need to pull the fabric so tight. Pre-lining is also helpful when using lightweight, thin, or delicate fabrics.

Blackout lining is recommended, not to block light (the boards do that!) but because it will hide any stains or discolorations of the wood, and it doesn't fray so the edges can be cut clean and even.

What You Will Need

- pattern paper
- ½-inch (1.3 cm) plywood (oriented strand board [OSB] can also be used.)
- lumber such as 1″ x 4″ or 1″ x 6″ boards
- spray adhesive
- polyester batting
- decorator fabric
- blackout lining
- pushpins
- heavy-duty stapler
- fabric glue
- welt cord
- gimp braid trim
- tools and hardware for building the frame
- tools and hardware for installation

Making a Pattern

Cornice board designs can be of any shape from scallops to stair-stepped right angles. Look in books, magazines, and online photo-sharing sites for inspiration. Often the fabric will inspire a design. A scale drawing on graph paper is a great first step and an easy way to experiment with shapes and styles before cutting the wood.

Using your measurements for the width and long and short points, draw at least half of the pattern of the finished cornice (face only, not the sides) on brown craft paper, or pattern paper. For this example kitchen freezer paper was used so that the fabric design would show through. The design followed the shape of the pattern motif.

Yardage Requirements

If using a print fabric, additional fabric may be needed to match the pattern motif.

Finished width to include returns and inside of returns + 4 inches (10.2 cm) ÷ fabric width = number of widths

Finished length plus top and inside of top + 4 inches (10.2 cm) = cut length

Number of widths x cut length ÷ 36 inches (91.4 cm) = number of yards (meters) needed

Additional yardage is needed to cut bias strips to make matching welt cord.

Constructing the Frame

The cornice board begins with a wooden frame. The most common size boards to use are 1" x 4" or 1" x 6", but smaller or larger boards can be used to fit the specific window. Be sure to allow enough of a projection for any other window treatments, window molding or drapery hardware. Make an allowance of 1 to 2 inches (2.5 to 5 cm) for the inside measurement (between the end boards) to clear the window frame or under treatments.

1. Cut a top board the finished width.

2. Cut the end boards the finished length minus the top board thickness (usually ¾ inch [1.8 cm]).

3. Trace the pattern onto plywood and cut using a jigsaw. Smooth rough edges with sand paper but don't overdo it—it will all be covered so perfection isn't necessary! **(A)**

4. Build the frame by nailing or screwing together the top board with two boards for each side, and then attach the plywood face. **(B)**

The shape of this cornice is inspired by the pattern motif.

A

A jigsaw is used to cut the plywood shape for the face of the cornice.

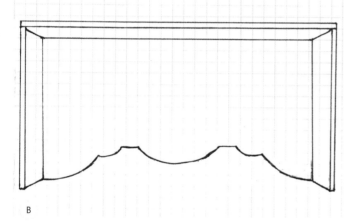

B

The cornice frame is made with boards on the top and sides, and a plywood face.

Upholstering the Frame

1. Cover the work surface with plastic or paper and lightly cover the face and sides with spray adhesive.

2. Cut a piece of polyester batting large enough to cover the cornice face and to wrap around the side. Press the batting over the wooden structure, sticking it to the adhesive.

Time saving tip: Fusible batting can be ironed to the wooden cornice. It will not have a strong bond, but it will stay in place until the fabric is stapled in place.

3. Trim away excess batting even with the top and bottom edges, and the back side edges. (C)

4. Cut and prepare fabric, seaming together if needed, matching patterns and pressing seams open.

5. Starting in the center, secure the top and bottom with several pushpins. Smooth out the fabric and pull gently and pin on the center of each side. Make sure the pattern motif is centered on the front and running even across the top. If a solid fabric is used make sure a full width is centered with seams equally spaced to the sides. (D)

6. Continue along the top and sides. For the bottom you will need to make relief cuts along the curves so the fabric will work around the shapes. Pull the fabric taut and even but not too tight.

7. Staple the bottom edge from the reverse side, removing pushpins as you go. You can work in sections starting at the center, pinning, clipping, and stapling, then continue across to the left and right.

C

Cut away excess batting even with the top and bottom edges.

D

Use pushpins along the edges, top, and sides to hold the fabric in place. Be sure to center the pattern motif.

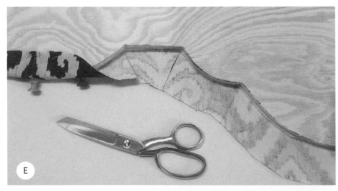

The fabric is clipped with "relief cuts," allowing it to wrap around cutouts and curves.

Staple the fabric to the reverse side.

Trim away excess fabric at the top corner, tuck under cut edges, and glue.

8. Pull and staple the fabric around the side and top boards, stapling to the inside. Clip and fold under cut edges at the top corner, adding glue under the edge. (G)

9. At the bottom sides, turn fabric under and staple but leave a little open space to hide the welt cord in the next step.

10. Cut and sew enough bias welt cord to cover the bottom and side edges. (See Chapter 3: Fundamental Techniques.) Cut and sew together additional 4-inch (10.2 cm)-wide bias strips. Sew the welt cord to the bias strip. The finished cord will have enough lip for stapling with no visible stitching. (H)

11. With the cornice face up, glue the welt cord to the bottom edge, starting in the middle and securing with pushpins. Allow the glue to dry. (I)

12. Turn the cornice over and secure the bias strip to the back, making relief cuts as needed to turn curves and corners. Staple in place. At each side, tuck the end of the cord under the fabric, folding over the end piece. Turn under all cut edges and glue. (J)

13. Cut a piece of blackout lining large enough to fit the inside, covering all exposed wood. Starting at the back, secure the lining wrong side up by stapling cardboard tack strip across the back, then flip the lining over the track strip so that it is right side up, trim as needed to fit, and glue to the back side. (K)

14. At the bottom edge, trace the design with pencil and cut slightly above the line. (L) Glue under the back and bottom edges. Finish the bottom edge by gluing gimp braid over the cut edge of the lining. (M)

15. Install using angle irons and screws. You will need an extra-long screwdriver or drill bit extension to reach the brackets.

Welt cord is sewn to a wide bias strip.

Glue the welt cord along the bottom edge. Add pushpins to hold it in place until the glue is set.

Make relief cuts in the bias strip and staple to the back of the cornice.

Cover the exposed wood with blackout lining.

Trace around the design with a pencil. Trim the lining ½ inch (1.3 cm) above the mark.

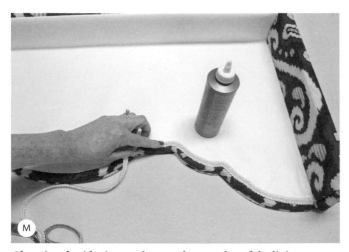

Glue gimp braid trim neatly over the cut edge of the lining.

The finished cornice board is ready to be installed.

UPHOLSTERED SOFT CORNICE WITH INSET BANDING

Cornice boards are typically constructed of wood, and while they are a beautiful style and fun to make, they can be quite heavy and difficult to install. A soft cornice, which uses a stiff interfacing instead of plywood, gives the same look with less weight, doesn't require as many woodworking tools, and can be attached to the mount board with staples or Velcro, allowing for more flexibility for difficult size and shapes of windows. This is mostly a no-sew project.

This is a lightweight version of a cornice, but it looks like it's made of wood.

Getting Started

Select fabrics that can that can be ironed with high heat and steam. Avoid thin, stretchy, or shiny fabrics, as they will not perform well with the adhesives and glue.

This project has a shaped inset band. Refer to Chapter 3: Fundamental Techniques for instructions.

What You Will Need

- decorator fabric
- blackout lining
- pattern paper
- stiff polyester interfacing like Peltex or Skirtex
- polyester fusible fleece
- fusible web like Wonder-Under
- fabric glue
- welt cord
- gimp braid trim
- wooden board

- Sealah double-sided adhesive flat shaper wire
- heavy-duty stapler
- pushpins
- tools and hardware for installation

Yardage Requirements

If using a print fabric, additional fabric may be needed to match the pattern motif.

Finished width + 4 inches (10.2 cm) ÷ fabric width = number of widths

Finished length + top + 4 inches (10.2 cm) = cut length

Number of widths x cut length ÷ 36 inches (91.4 cm) = number of yards (meters) needed

Additional yardage is needed for bias strips for welt cord.

For this project, the reverse sides of the returns are covered in lining. If your cornice has an angled design, you may want to cover the inside of the return areas with face fabric because it may show when viewed from below. Allow extra to the width when estimating the yardage.

Making an Upholstered Soft Cornice with Inset Banding

1. Draw a pattern using the same techniques as for the wood cornice. Make the finished size ½ inch (1.3 cm) wider to allow for take-up of the thick layers. At the top and sides, add the size of the board to the pattern, making a cutout at the left and right top corners. (A)

2. Glue inset banding to the face fabric using the pattern and rulers to make sure it is lined up properly. Banding or other trims can also be added later, after the cornice is constructed but before board mounting. (B)

3. Use the pattern to draw and cut one each of Peltex, fusible fleece, and adhesive web.

4. With the fabric face down, top with the fleece, adhesive side down. Iron the fleece to the fabric, centering pattern motifs and keeping the fabric neat and flat. Use a "press cloth" (a scrap of cotton lining or muslin) so the fleece will not stick to the iron. After the fleece is attached, turn the fabric over and press from the front. Try to use only one piece of fleece. If your project is larger than the fleece, butt pieces together at the board line, or returns, but not in the center front of the cornice. (C)

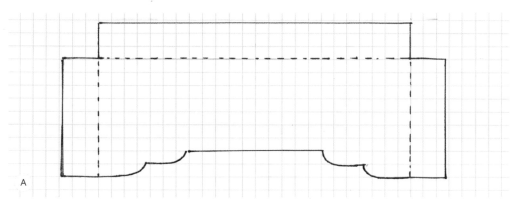

A

Draw the pattern, adding for the returns and top.

C

Apply fusible fleece to the back of the face fabric.

B

Shaped banding is glued to the fabric.

Apply fusible web to the back of the Peltex and peel away the paper backing.

Place the Peltex adhesive side down over the fleece.

Iron the Peltex to the fleece, joining them together.

5. Apply the fusible web to the back of the Peltex by ironing with the paper-backing side up. After it is completely ironed and cooled, peel away the paper backing. You can butt together pieces of the fusible web if one whole piece is not large enough. (D)

6. Place the Peltex with the adhesive backing to the fleece, which is attached to the back of the face fabric. Line up the pieces so the shapes match. (E) Iron the pieces together using a press cloth. (F)

7. Trim away excess fabric along the bottom edge to 1½ to 2 inches (3.8 to 5 cm). Glue the cut edges to the back of the Peltex using fabric glue. Make relief cuts at the corners, and clip around curves as needed. Pin in place and let dry. (G)

8. Make bias-covered welt cord. Cut additional strips of fabric on the bias 2½ inches (6.4 cm) wide, join the pieces together, and sew to the welt cord, getting close so all the stitching is hidden. (H) This will be used as a facing along the reverse of the cornice. (I)

9. Glue the welt cord along the bottom edge, following the design. Make sure no stitching shows. Pin and let dry. (J)

10. Turn the piece over and glue the facing to the back, making relief cuts and clipping as needed. (K) The shape of this cornice has sharp corners, which require a deep relief cut. Small patches of matching fabric are used to cover the corners. (L)

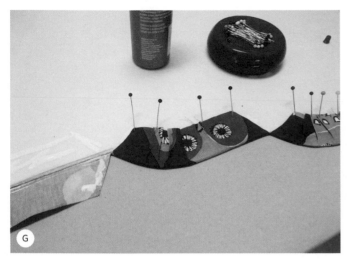

Trim away excess fabric at the bottom edge, leaving enough extra fabric to turn under and glue to the back.

Sew a bias strip to the welt cord, getting close the cord to hide the stitching.

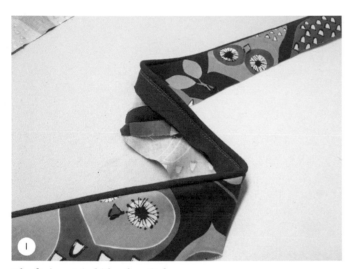

The facing strip hides the stitches.

Glue the welt cord to the bottom edge.

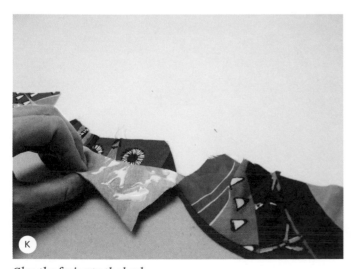

Glue the facing to the back.

A small patch of matching fabric covers the corner relief cut.

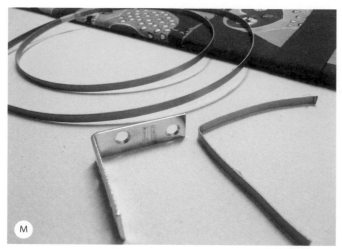

Use Sealah shaper or L-brackets to create a right angle at each side return.

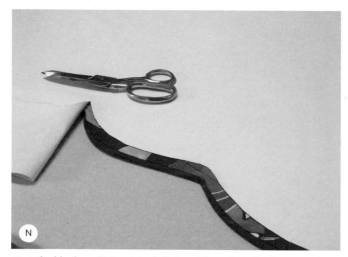

Cut the blackout lining 1 inch (2.5 cm) less than the bottom edge.

Turn the face fabric over the sides and cover the cut edges with lining.

11. Add pieces of Sealah double-sided adhesive flat shaper wire to the bottom edges at each return, inset about 2 inches (5 cm) from the bottom. This will let you shape the return at a right angle. If you don't have this product, you can attach an L-bracket with double-sided tape or pieces of florist wire. The goal is to add something that will create a right angle for the return. (M)

12. Cover the back with blackout lining. Trim the lining 1 inch (2.5 cm) shorter on the back bottom edge. (N) At each side, turn over the face fabric and glue to the Peltex, and then turn under the lining and glue. (O)

13. Glue gimp braid over the cut edge of the lining on the back, at the bottom of the cornice. (P)

14. At each end, fold over the size needed for the return, and press with heat and steam. This will help the cornice bend into shape. Repeat for the top.

15. Cover the mounting board with lining. Staple the soft cornice to the board (Q), turning under the cut edges and trimming away excess fabric. (R) If areas are bulky, trim away Peltex or fleece to fit the board. Staple across the back edge of the board and glue the top edges. (S)

16. Install to the wall using L-brackets. (See Chapter 7: Installing Window Treatments.)

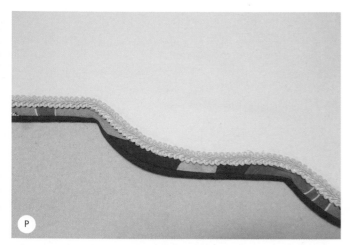

Glue gimp braid over the cut edge of the lining.

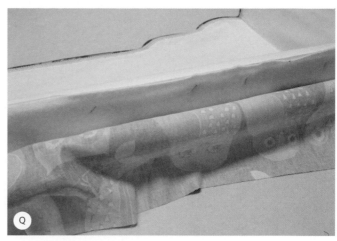

Staple the Peltex and fleece at the top of the board.

Cut away excess fabric at the corners.

Turn under the cut edges, glue, and hold in place with pushpins until the glue dries.

Contrast welt cord and banding are eye-catching details.

INSTALLING WINDOW TREATMENTS

You have picked out the perfect fabrics, designed and constructed a beautiful window treatment, and now it's time to get it up on the window! Often this is a very simple task using basic tools, but some projects, such as two-story windows, require extra time, effort, and specialty equipment.

In this section you will learn the basics of board mounting, traverse hardware, and cord safety. You will learn not only how to put curtains up on the window but also tricks for dressing and training fabrics for a fabulous finish!

Installation is the final step, but it's not something that just happens at the end of the project. Start thinking about and planning the installation from the very beginning when you measure and select fabrics and hardware, and throughout the process of sewing and finishing. Being prepared and ready for the installation is the key to a successful and beautiful finished window treatment.

Types of Hardware

There are many styles and types of hardware, from simple utility rods to elaborate decorative poles. Choosing the best hardware for your project is based on the use and purpose of the window treatment. If you want to open and close curtains, purchase traversing hardware. For stationary curtains, a simple extension rod can be used.

With decorative hardware, the style and finish are important parts of the overall design. Examples include painted or stained wood, metal, iron, and even glass and acrylic in traditional and contemporary designs.

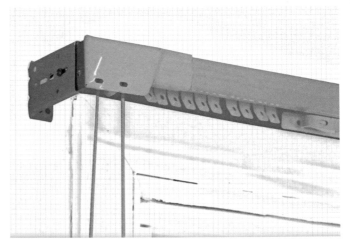

Use a heavy-duty traverse rod for functional curtains.

The right hardware makes a statement! This rod made with industrial pipe is perfect for a modern loft. The same curtain would look much different with a traditional wooden pole rod.

LEFT *This photo with the swag and drapery is an illustration of a two-story window.*

Mounting Boards

Many window treatments are board mounted. This is one of the most common ways to install top treatments and valances, but curtains and shades can also be mounted to boards.

Boards should be covered or painted so they look neat and clean, and secured to the wall or window trim with L-brackets. Use a bracket that is larger than half the board projection. For example, use at least a 2-inch (5 cm) bracket to install a 3½-inch (8.9 cm) board.

The brackets are installed to the wall and the board is set on top, and then fastened with screws. Use an appropriate amount of brackets for the size and weight of the window treatment. There should be a bracket placed every 36 to 48 inches (91.4 to 122 cm).

The window treatment can be stapled to the board or attached with hook-and-loop tape so it can be removed. When stapling the window treatment directly to the board, make sure all the staples and cut edges are covered. This is especially important if the top of the board can be viewed from a balcony or stairway. The following instructions will show you several different ways to cover mount boards.

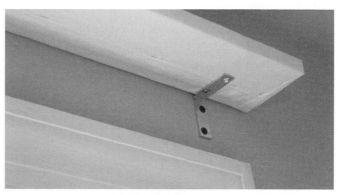

Use L-brackets to install mount boards.

COVERING A BASIC MOUNT BOARD

1. Cut a piece of fabric large enough to wrap around the board and overlap 1 inch (2.5 cm) the length of the board plus 4 inches (10.2 cm). Wrap the fabric over each end and staple.

2. Wrap the fabric over the top, folding corners in neatly and staple.

3. Overlap the fabric and staple to finish.

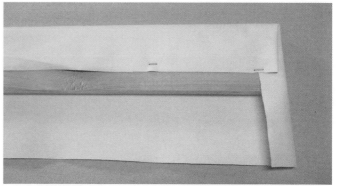

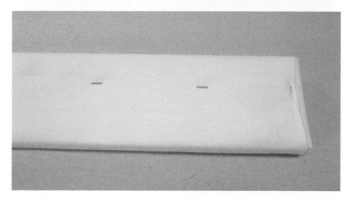

Attaching to a Mount Board: Option 1

1. Cover the board with matching fabric and staple the window treatment to the top. (A)

2. Cut a piece of matching fabric large enough to wrap around and 2 inches (5 cm) longer than the board. Place the fabric face down along the front edge and staple to the board using cardboard tack strip. Fold over each end and staple. (B)

3. Flip the fabric over the tack strip. (C) The tack strip creates a crisp and even edge. (D)

4. Fold under the cut edges and staple to the back edge of the board. The staples will be on the edge that is against the wall.

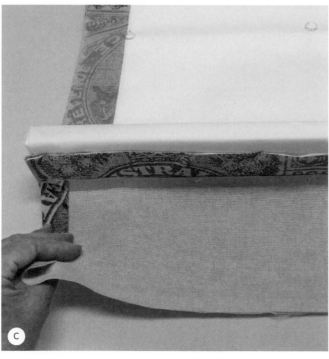

Attaching to a Mount Board: Option 2

1. Cover each end of the board with fabric. (A)

2. Staple the window treatment on top of the board. This window treatment wraps around the ends. (B)

3. Staple covered welt cord to the top front edge. This is optional; you can continue without welt cord. (C)

4. Cut a piece of matching fabric large enough to cover the top and wrap entirely around the board plus extra on each end to turn under. Staple face down with cardboard tack strip. (D)

5. Fold the fabric under at each end and glue under the fold, or use a double-sided adhesive tape to finish the ends. (E)

6. Continue wrapping the fabric around the board to the opposite edge, hidden under the back of the window treatment. Tuck under the cut edges and staple. (F)

Another option for mounting to boards is to sew a band to the top. You can then staple the band to a covered board, or attach with hook-and-loop tape. In the example at right, the banding is sewn to a pleated valance, but it can also be used for shades, swags, jabots, and board-mounted curtains. Be sure to add for the seam allowance when marking and cutting the finished length of the window treatment.

SEWING A TOP BAND FOR BOARD MOUNTING

1. Cut a strip of matching fabric 3½ inches (8.9 cm) by the finished size needed plus 2 inches (5 cm). Use a serger or an overcast stitch to finish one long edge.

2. Place the strip face down and pin the cut edge (not the serged edge) to the top, turning under 1 inch (2.5 cm) on each end to the back. Sew to the top using a ½-inch (1.3 cm) seam allowance. (A)

3. Fold the banding up and press from the front. (B)

4. Turn the window treatment face down. Add fabric glue to the top along the seam allowance. (C)

5. Fold the band over the glue and press. The glue will hold the banding in place until it is sewn. This is easier than pinning! (D)

6. Sew across the banding from the top. (E)

7. At each end, fold over the return allowance and stitch at a 45-degree angle across the band to create a square corner. (F) (G)

8. Sew loop strip to the underside of the band. Hook strip is stapled to the board. (H)

When installing stationary curtains under board-mounted valances, screw eyes can be added under the board for drapery pins.

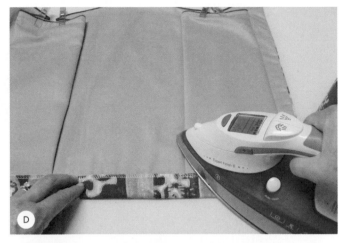

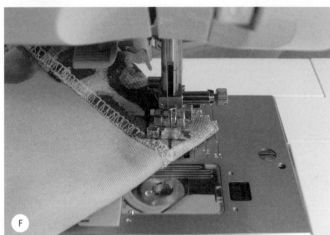

Installation Tools and Tips

The key to a successful installation is preparation and patience. Every window is unique and every window treatment is different. You might be installing hardware into walls with wood studs and sheetrock or plaster and lathe, wood, metal, or concrete.

Some styles, such as cornice boards, can be tricky to install because of the limited space between the front of the cornice and the wall. An extension is needed on the drill to reach up into the tight space to screw the brackets to the mount board. Two-story windows or windows over stairways will need extension ladders and in some cases mechanical lifts to complete the installation.

Be aware of what might be inside the wall, such as water pipes and electrical wires, and glass when installing on doors.

Installing window treatments is often a job that is best left to a professional who has the knowledge and experience to complete the job safely and properly. The end goal is to have window treatments that will function easily and hang beautifully for years and years.

But don't be intimidated! Many window treatments are easy to install, and you will feel quite accomplished when you step back and admire your new window dressings.

Before you begin the installation, put together a kit with all the tools and hardware that you will need. Typical items you will need include a ladder, screws, drill and drill bits, tape measure, level, awl, and pencil. Different surfaces require different types of screws, anchors, and fasteners. It's best to use Phillips or hex-head screws with the appropriate driver for your drill or screwdriver.

Familiarize yourself with the manufacturer's instructions and preassemble the hardware if necessary.

Measure and mark for the bracket placement based on the size of the window treatment. Use an awl to poke gently into the wall to see whether it is solid or hollow. You can also drill a small hole first, before setting screws—this is an important step on hollow walls or doors. Be sure to use a drill bit that is smaller than the screw size.

Continue installing the hardware, checking to make sure it is level. Sometimes the hardware is level but the ceiling or floor is not! Make subtle adjustments to make the window treatment appear level to the eye.

Adjust cord-draw traverse rods at the back of the master carriers, pulling out the cord to the length needed, setting the master carriers to the center, and then cutting off and knotting the cord. Once the cord is the correct length, set the cord to a fixed position by looping it over the small hook on the opposite carrier.

On window coverings with cords, be sure to follow the manufacturer's instructions for installing safety devices, and use them properly. Read any attached warning labels. It is best practice to use only cord-free window coverings in homes where children live or visit. Safety first, decorating second!

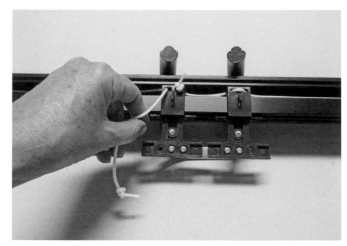

Pull out the cords to the length needed, setting the master carriers into the correct position.

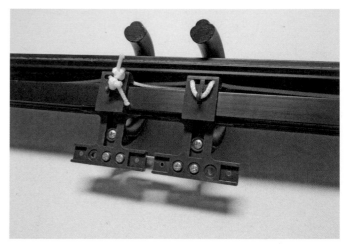

Set the position by looping the cord under the hook.

Helpful Tips

- Add double-sided tape to the back of brackets to temporarily hold the bracket to the wall. This will free up your hands for holding screws and drilling.

- Use silicone spray to lubricate traverse rods, and wipe it along the top of decorative poles so rings move back and forth easier.

- A drill with a magnetic driver will help prevent screws from slipping away and dropping to the floor.

- Make a cardboard template for bracket placement when there are multiple windows of the same size and using the same hardware.

- Wear a tool apron.

- Secure returns on curtains and valances by installing a tenterhook or screw eye in the wall for the pin hook (as shown in photos).

Use a tenterhook to hold the return.

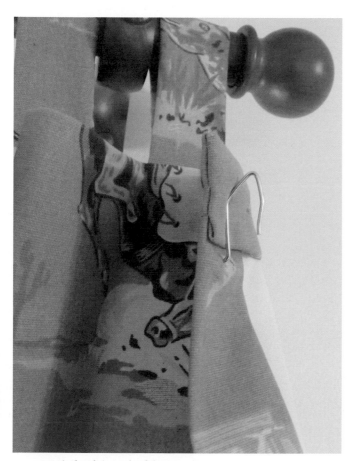

Insert a pin hook into the fabric at the return and hook over the tenterhook.

Curtains look best when the fabric returns to the wall.

Hanging and Dressing Window Treatments

After the window treatment is installed, it will need to be dressed to neaten the fold and drape of the fabric. To dress curtains, smooth the fabric with your hands and use a steamer to remove wrinkles. An oven mitt can be worn and the fabric lightly pressed against the mitt for more stubborn wrinkles.

On traverse rods with curtains where the hardware is behind the top heading, crease the spaces between the pleats forward. On decorative rods where the top heading is below the rings, the spaces between pleats can be creased to the back or brought forward.

Open the curtains to the side and work down each pleat, using your hands to straighten. After the curtains are arranged neatly, tie wide strips of muslin around the curtain from the top to the bottom, holding the curtain together. Tie the bands snug but not too tight or they will crease the fabric. Let the curtains stay bound overnight or for a few days. This will train the folds.

For Roman shades, pull up to the highest position and smooth horizontally with your hands, creating even folds. Steam and let the shade stay in this position overnight. This will help the fabric refold neatly.

Manipulate the fabric on valances and top treatments by smoothing by hand and arranging pleats and folds to the desired look. A tag or tacking gun can be used to control flare by tacking inside pleats and folds.

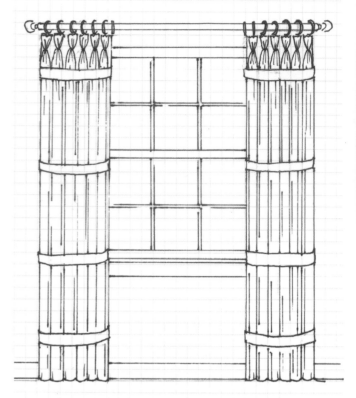

Wrap the installed curtains with muslin bands to train the folds.

Use a tag or tacking gun to control flare.

Glossary of Common Terms and Definitions

Bead weight (aka sausage weight)—tiny weights that are encased inside a woven strip and added to the bottom curtains for an even weight across the entire hem. Bead weight can also be covered and used in place of welt cord in seams.

Blackout—a lining material that has been treated to block all light. Look for a three-pass blackout material for complete light blocking.

Board mount—installing a window treatment to a top board that is then secured to the wall.

Buckram—traditionally a woven cotton cloth stiffened with starch (aka crinoline), but modern versions can be made from polyester or heavy paper. Used to add structure in curtain and valance headings for crisp pleats. Buckram is available in different widths and sew-on or iron-on. The most common width is 4 inches (10.2 cm).

Bump cloth—a very heavy blanket-like interlining commonly used in silk for a luxurious finish.

Curtain or drapery panel—a panel is one piece of a curtain or drapery hung at the window. Panels can be single or multiple widths of fabric sewn together.

Decorative hardware—wooden or metal pole rods used for installing curtains and valances.

Dim out—also called thermal lining, this material has a suede-like surface that helps to diffuse light.

Finial—a decorative detail added to the end of pole rods.

French blackout—a method for creating blackout using face fabric layered with interlining, black lining, and an outer lining.

Fullness—the amount of extra fabric width needed to create pleats or gathers in a window treatment in relation to the size of the window or rod. A common fullness ratio used in window treatments is to multiple two and a half times the rod width.

Hand—the way a fabric feels when touched and draped.

Heading—the hem at the top of a drapery or valance that is shirred or pleated. A heading often has buckram, shirring tape, grommets, or other details to create a specific style.

Headrail—any system used to operate a blind or shade.

Interlining—usually flannel but can be any fabric that is sandwiched between the face fabric and lining.

Lining—a cotton, polyester and cotton blend, or polyester fabric used to cover the reverse side of a window treatment. Look for a lining material that is specifically finished for window treatments; they will perform better than other fabrics. Two common brands in the United States are Hanes Fabrics and Rockland Industries. Most common colors of lining are white, ivory, and khaki.

Medallions—decorative posts or knobs used at the top of draped window treatments or for tiebacks.

Railroading fabric—placing fabric so that it runs down the bolt instead of side to side. This is common in upholstery or when making valances and top treatments to eliminate seams. Some fabrics are printed with this orientation specifically for upholstery.

Repeat—how often the pattern motif on a fabric is duplicated. There are horizontal and vertical pattern repeats.

Return—the area on window treatments that wraps around the hardware or board flush to the wall to cover the projection.

Selvage—the finished edges along the length of the fabric.

Tabling—a term used in the workroom to describe laying out fabrics, measuring, and finishing pieces of a window treatment on the worktable.

Valance—a decorative window treatment that dresses the top of the window. A valance can be plain, pleated, shirred, or a swag style.

Weight tape—square weights sewn into a wide tape, most commonly used in hems of stage curtains and other heavy, large projects.

Weights—metal pieces that are square, round, or triangular in shape and added to hems and seams to help window treatments hang properly. Traditionally, weights are made of lead but newer versions are made of non-lead metal compounds and are safer for the environment.

Gallery

Thank you to the following designers for providing the beautiful interior photographs of their window treatments for this book.

Decorating Den Interiors / Barbara Elliott and Jennifer Ward Woods

Decorating Den Interiors / Cathi Lloyd

Decorating Den Interiors / Sandy Kozar

Decorating Den Interiors / Heidi Sowatsky

Decorating Den Interiors / Shawn Strok

Decorating Den Interiors / Lois Pade

Decorating Den Interiors / Terry Varner

Decorating Den Interiors / Barbara Tabak

*Decorating Den Interiors /
Sandy Kozar*

*Decorating Den Interiors / Barbara Elliott and
Jennifer Ward Woods*

Decorating Den Interiors / Suzan Wemlinger

*Decorating Den Interiors /
Diana Apgar*

Decorating Den Interiors / Bonnie Pressley

Decorating Den Interiors / Cathi Lloyd

Heather Hannick Designs, constructed and installed by Windows and More by Chrystal, Chrystal Younger

Decorating Den Interiors / Diana Apgar

Decorating Den Interiors / Tonie VanderHulst

Decorating Den Interiors / Suzan Wemlinger

Resources

FABRICS, SEWING AND WORKROOM SUPPLIES

DraperySupplies.com
HanesFabrics.com
HomeSew.com
HomeSewingDepot.com
Joann.com
MaryJos.com
NancysNotions.com
RowleyCompany.com
Textol.com
Wawak.com

ADHESIVE TAPES

Dofix.com
Jodeesinc.com
Kwikaffix.com
Millenniumtape.com
DonnaSkufis.com

PROFESSIONAL WINDOW TREATMENT PATTERNS

Mfay.com
PateMeadows.com
PatternsPlus.com

HARDWARE

HelserBrothers.com
SafeTShade.com
UnitedSupplyCo.com

EDUCATION

Craftsy.com
DraperyandDesign.com
HomeDecGal.com
TheWorkroomChannel.com

About the Author

Susan Woodcock owns HomeDecGal.com, a how-to sewing and decorating resource and workroom in western North Carolina. She began teaching professionally in 2003, and is currently a Craftsy.com instructor. She has also worked in marketing and brand management, and is co-producer of the Custom Workroom Conference with her husband, Rodger Walker. She credits her mother for teaching her to sew, leading to a career of creativity.

Design and Sketch Your Own Curtains

Index